Fictions and Ceremonies

Representations
of Popular Experience

Fictions and Ceremonies

Representations of Popular Experience

David Chaney

St. Martin's Press · New York

ISBN 0-312-28814-X

Library of Congress Cataloging in Publication Data

Chaney, David C
    Fictions and ceremonies.

    Bibliography: p.
    Includes index.
    1. Popular culture.   2. Arts and society.
    3. Communication in art.   I. Title.

NX180.S6C43   1979   301.2'1   78-31437
ISBN 0-312-28814-X

Contents

Preface

This book has matured slowly over several years, the constituent chapters were written independently of each other but now combine to form a cumulative argument. As it has been written while teaching a course in cultural studies I am very conscious of my debts to several generations of students — both for their tolerance of imperfectly thought-out arguments being thrust upon them, and for their occasionally enthusiastic willingness to tackle new ideas. A substantial proportion of the book was written while spending sabbatical leave at the Annenberg School of Communications at the University of Philadelphia. I am grateful to George Gerbner and my friends there for the stimulating intellectual environment they provided, and in particular to Larry Gross and Dan Schiller for their sympathetic encouragement that the project was worth doing and could be accomplished. All my friends at Durham have endured garbled reports either in seminars or in conversation of what I have been trying to get down on paper; I am grateful to them all. In particular I must mention those graduate students who have worked with me over the past few years. It is invidious to name individuals but Tom Owen's work on constructivism has had an enormous influence on my ideas, Margy Cockburn has consistently helped and encouraged with sense and sensitivity, and Pam Thomas has understood the epigraph and its implications.

I dedicate the book to Judith and Sophie who have been remarkably tolerant of the egocentricity of intellectual conceit.

'The first duty in life is to be as artificial as possible.'   Oscar Wilde

1

Taking Popular Art Seriously

The Project

I did think for some time of using this chapter title for the whole book but was dissuaded. I have retained it for this introductory chapter because it provides a useful peg for points relevant to the organization of my work. The idea for this title came to me at the end of a lecture on post-revolutionary art and culture in China given at the University of Durham. In trying to show a connection between the ideological character of a refusal in contemporary China to discriminate between 'high' and popular art, the lecturer summarized art as political practice by saying that the Chinese take popular art seriously in a way that is not generally done in capitalist societies. This stimulus should not be taken as an indication that what follows is a trenchant exposition of Maoist thought; rather that the phrase seems to me to provoke a number of fundamental questions. To take popular art seriously implies the possibility both of identifying 'popular' and of elucidating an attitude of seriousness in relation to the arts.

Beginning with the first point, I believe it to be of only limited utility to try to identify popular art through features of performances that may generally be agreed to be popular, i.e. derive a stylistic essence of 'popular-ness'. Such a definitional perspective is limited because its initial impetus is provided by instances from particular cultural and historical contexts. However determined the author may be to transcend the limitations of his starting-point he is necessarily engaged in constructing a typology based upon an initial discrimination. A recent example is provided by John Cawelti's book (1976) which despite its many strengths always seems a fragile construct — it rests on fundamental judgments about distinctions between popular and serious which are culturally *a priori*, not analytically derived. In order to avoid constituting our topic by the instances we choose, popular has to be understood through constitutive social relations of production. Popular can be assumed to be those styles of expressive symbolism primarily intended for anonymous and/or heterogeneous audiences. Work which is designed to correspond to or is later incorporated into academic canons of merit may also be 'popular' in the sense that it is

7

attended to by large numbers of people, but academic canons are not derived from popular styles (even in an explicitly populist culture such as contemporary China it is tendentious to claim that academic standards are derived from popular styles). Popular art is that work produced to appeal to a perceived audience in terms of their, probably, unarticulated expectations rather than correspond to formal features derived from traditional or academic conventions. An implication of this assertion is that the core difference between capitalist and socialist societies in relation to popular art must lie in how 'perceptions' of audiences are arrived at rather than in some aesthetic essence of the meaning of popular.

In saying that popular art is intended for anonymous audiences I mean that the audience is not defined by particular racial, cultural or geographical affiliations — it may well consist entirely of friends of the author (performer) but the popular artist would usually consider such a situation an instance of a lack of success (popularity). The obvious objection to this criterion is provided by an example such as jazz where the music was and is specifically oriented (as in 'race records') to a particular racial/cultural audience. Black music in North America is a good instance of a popular art form with a very strong identification with a particular segment of the total possible audience; and precisely because this segment is hierarchically subordinate in the general social structure the art form that can most clearly be identified as 'theirs' becomes a badge of identity, a display of alternative cultural values and something inaccessible to other, more privileged, segments of the population (see Jones 1967 for a strident articulation of these and related claims). It is not my intention here to assess the empirical validity of these claims (even assuming that such validity is assessible), but merely to note in passing how such an ideology of cultural privacy is continually being vitiated by the temptations of the white-dominated music industry to 'popularize' performances for large cash rewards both for records and for live performances. Given competing demands it is unsurprising that a professional split between private music for insiders and public music for squares first noted sociologically by Howard Becker (1963) developed; or that in time the more fervent advocates of cultural autonomy should attempt to resolve the pressures of popularization through forcing the performance to be increasingly inaccessible (and in this way denying the popularity although not the populism of the form; both of these strands are brought out in Russell's (1973) biography of Charlie Parker). One cannot deny the significance of local affiliations in the case of jazz, and many other popular art forms, but it is precisely because the cultural isolation of those affiliations cannot be sustained, because the anonymous audience is the potential patron of any performance, that styles of taste in popular art are only approximate markers of statuses and roles.

The anonymity of the audience is often taken to be a consequence of size, and it is often true that the scale of popularity is a sufficient if not necessary guarantee of anonymity. More significantly it can be argued that the scale, heterogeneity and anonymity of audiences for popular art ensure that it is characteristically produced collectively rather than individually; in part because the scale of demand, and the uncertainty of success, means that the work cannot afford the scrupulousness of individual self-consciousness. Other reasons apply in the case of 'live' entertainment, such as football and music hall, which are self-evidently collaborative enterprises. However, even when one is dealing with more individualized performances, where there is a recognizable *auteur* — as in the case of popular fiction, or more arguably the popular film, — their authority is articulated through essential collaborators such as editors, agents and distributors (it may be useful to apply the common-sense distinction between directors and producers to media other than film). An objection is that in this case it is very hard to think of performances that are not collaborative in that art, as we understand it, must be at least sponsored if not sold and therefore involves the activities of more than the artist (see the discussion in Becker 1974). At this point definitional discussion becomes unnecessary, it is sufficient to note that popular art is in general less easily identified as the work of an individual and is more usually articulated through collaborative interaction.

The rationale for collaborative industry in this area has in capitalist societies been the hope that the ensuing performances will attract sufficient attention to provide their producers with adequate, even specta-cular, financial rewards. It is not necessary to assume that this marketing of popular art as negotiable commodity is a defining feature, one can phrase the rationale more generally and say that popular art is produced *for* an audience. One might say that the producers are oriented to popular esteem however that is expressed. This does not mean that producers cannot invest the project with wit, invention and originality (artifice) or that they cannot be passionately convinced that this is the correct way of artistically articulating an idea (for an example picked at random see Anita Loos 1974). The search for popularity is not antithetical to holding standards of style and taste, but the commitment to such standards is to making ideas work in a public manner. It may be dispiriting for Satie to have his work rejected as inaccessible but it does not negate the enterprise; popular art is ephemeral because it is designed for its time — it may succeed in a different context either through innate style, charm, nostalgia or whatever — but it makes no sense to say that it was designed for posterity. One can extend this point by saying in the production of popular art, while it is conventional, indeed very often highly stylized, the forms used are unofficial. For all the reasons of the characteristic features of popular art given so far, the canons of successful styles are not canonized as legitimate knowledge — they are not taught as a civilizing influence and are only rarely sufficiently organized to be taught as professional skills; the forms of popular art are non-official because they are the means of expression used rather than the means a visitor from another culture might suppose are the official norms.

The social relations of production of popular art-work, whatever the particular organizational features of any medium, are therefore instances of the collective manufacture of unofficial public performances for anonymous audiences. These relations of production ensure that performances are so embedded in their context that they provide an important part of the ways a public can conceptualize its own activities — they are a vocabulary of collective consciousness. It may be that there is an 'objective reality' such as the exhaustion of natural resources or the accumulation of productive capital in the control of a few immense corporations and that these processes determine the forms of consciousness possible in any period; but the forms of public consciousness are not explicable in terms of the 'laws' which govern such 'reality'. This is because public consciousness involves infinitely reflective awareness and mystification. The 'language' within which we situate the 'vocabulary' of particular performances is made up of the ways in which collective, unofficial and anonymous etc., are understood in any particular society. Another way of putting this point is to say that the numinous realm of 'public' knowledge is those ways we characterize each other. The performances of popular art are instances of characterization which inevitably utilize themselves as evidence, as tangible signs of common experience. It is impossible to think that popular art can exist unless the members of a society feel a need to characterize their social context as something potentially alien to themselves. The anonymity and fluidity of urban society is therefore an extremely common subject of the narrative dramas of popular art but is itself a prerequisite before those dramas can be produced.

In the course of this book I several times draw an analogy between the epistemological stance of popular art and the activities of an ethnographer. I hope it will become apparent that the analogy is not coincidental. In this case the analogy derives from the way the ethnographer attempts to show the flux of communal process from his stance as privileged observer, analogous to the previous argument that a prerequisite of popular art is a documentary impulse — the concern to show the community in process. The difference between popular art and ethnography is that the performances of the former cannot in general claim access to a privileged (scientific) stance; indeed their reports make up the public sphere and give it a tangibility it otherwise could not possess. The difference between popular art and private (personal) experience is that although the audience is the public sphere which provides the imagery for popular performances, the imagery in art is staged. The performances are provided by specialists for acceptance or rejection; therefore the circularity in the concept of public is not oppressive because the relations of production distance narrative dramas. Popular art remains vicarious while the sense of public is recognized to be a fiction. When the members of an audience take their collective identity as imposing responsibilities and legitimate demands on their personal self-conceptions, as for example when members of a football crowd act out their status as folk-devils, then the crowd becomes — in the eyes of those concerned to maintain social order — a mob. Revolutions, as the most spectacular genre of popular art, require that street dramas become transposed from reportable events to performances with demands upon participants.

I have argued that it is more fruitful to locate the force of popular art in the social relations of production than by sifting through a sample of performances for essential features. It may seem surprising, therefore, that my approach to productive relationships does not work through organizational details (an interesting precursor of a small tradition of studies of the inter-relationships between organizational form and cultural style is provided by Elliott 1973). My reason is that I wish to elucidate the 'sensibility' of productive industry — the context or framework within which activities are organized in producing specific performances: 'It is too simple to see these defining variables simply in terms of constraints. . . . The other part, which we particularly wish to stress, is their ability to suggest and in some sense create i.e. implicate. This seems to happen through the shared understandings current in the different social contexts of media production' (Elliott and Chaney 1969 p.370). The status of empirical examples is necessarily arbitrary in this account. How would I defend my selection of illustrative detail, and what evidence would one produce to dispute the selection? The damaging point might be made that my account depends upon pointing to examples of popular art — an approach I initially repudiated. These are real objections and they can only be substantively answered in the course of the study. At this point I can only say that as we cannot begin with an authoritative and final list of definitional features, any set of characteristics we use will be approximate and the members of the set will shift in significance with changes of context. Thus while it is sensible to expect modification, the account could only be crucially undermined by someone producing an era or genre of popular art in which features of the social relations of production I have mentioned were importantly irrelevant and inappropriate. The important point is that in the ensuing debate the initial concern would be with the socially constitutive features that men take (or are forced to take) seriously when designing imagery in recreation relevant to themselves and their peers.

A further objection to my analytic stance is that it is crippled by a failure to emphasize the fact that historically the productive relations discussed have been situated in a hierarchically stratified social order. To take just one example, the public sphere mentioned above is not co-terminous with the nation-state or equally accessible to every member of that nation. The development of the public was a central feature of the growth of bourgeois society, and as such the public is always rooted in contradiction. The claim of an objective attitude to social experience is that there are facts (news) which can be reported and which should constitute the parameters of rational discourse. This claim is mystifying in its own terms because there is no fundamental logic to social experience to which all men must finally assent; rather 'knowledge' is selective and persuasive — it is an organization of sense which is informed by the values, beliefs and expectations of those who share a commitment to a certain version of reality. The hegemonic impulse of bourgeois elites is to present the public sphere as the unquestioned and unquestionable realm of facts discovered and discoverable, and yet the organization of knowledge through which bourgeois culture is articulated is necessarily related to the historical and cultural context. Thus public consciousness is never homogeneous, it stretches through a number of cultural 'levels' and across a huge gamut of tastes and styles. The heterogeneity of public experience is a display of cultural democratization but for this very reason always a potential source of anarchic cultural fragmentation. Therefore the production of popular art is always an area of shifting and more or less explicit modes of social control providing a crucial tension over expectations, aspirations and denial.

Although I have emphasized the constitutive significance of productive relationships, the recognition of historical contextualism should remind us that the fictions created are versions of reality. The stories told may be functional for the preservation of social order or may be utilized as vehicles for dissent and objection. In both cases the performances can be interpreted as ideological accounts, as stories which need annotation. The arguments developed in this book are not instances of annotative interpretations in that sense but are not opposed to such analyses. Rather, my concern is to deepen our grasp of ideological structure by moving beyond fiction as something meaningful through purporting to be pictorial representation, to *a grasp of narrative as stories which are tellable.* In the latter sense ideology is not a distorted report but certain limiting presuppositions on how to report. I therefore believe that by starting with the institutional rationality of popular art we are directly entering the ways in which cultural practices are competing forms of life. This assumption does not mean that hierarchical tension is an integral feature of *any* form of social organization, and thus one can imagine a popular art not structured by class conflict, but I do not know of an instance of such a popular art in preceding or contemporary society.

I have been commenting on the possibility of an alternative approach to the study of popular art than that conventional in studies that begin with thematic or stylistic features of popular cultural performances. The central flaw with the latter approach is that it provides for an interpretive stance whose ultimate aspiration is a critical exegesis of 'meanings', so that the performances can be explored as a layered set of puzzles.

Therefore any form of critical stance assumes as a minimum that the 'real' content of a performance, that which is 'going on', is not self-evident — particularly when the critic is concerned with performances, for example orchestral music, in which the narrative structure is at best highly symbolized. A critical stance is therefore initially descriptive — report of what the performance is like (about) — but then aspires to account for the import of described features: 'Literary-critical, linguistic and stylistic methods of analysis are, by contrast, more useful in penetrating the latent meanings of a text, and they preserve something of the complexity of language and connotation which has to be sacrificed in content analysis in order to achieve high validation' (Smith *et al.* 1975 p.15). Literary criticism is usually taken to be the paradigmatic example of a critical approach. It is surprising that in such an explicitly theoretical discipline there should be so little discussion of issues such as the analyst's warrant for his interpretive ventures — for whom does he make his judgements of import and how does he judge the strengths of competing interpretations? (Interestingly, this provides another instance of potential analogies between criticism and ethnography, in this case naive criticism and naive ethnography.) If a critic should want to take up the theoretical grounds of his own work he would have to consider the ways in which his activity makes his subject possible. I wish to undercut a critical emphasis upon the performance (text) and concentrate upon the milieu in which that performance becomes conceivable.

It is possibly because his book is effectively non-academic and more successfully witty and urbane than the majority of work in this field that Cockburn's introduction to his study of best-sellers is particularly germane. Seeking to defend his account against a charge of inappropriate seriousness towards ephemeral topics, Cockburn (1972 pp.2-3) argues that persistent popularity is a sufficient demonstration of public needs: 'You cannot deny that if Book X was what a huge majority of book-buyers and book-borrowers wanted to buy or borrow in a given year, or over a period of years, then Book X satisfied a need, and expressed and realized emotions and attitudes to life which the buyers and borrowers did not find expressed or realized elsewhere'. Given that this functional relationship between author and public exists it must depend upon 'the existence of a *rapport,* a sympathy — in the exact sense of the word — between the conscious or unconscious mind of the reader and that of the author;' (*op. cit.* p.11). But in saying this Cockburn indicates that the criteria of significance he presumes (whether or not they are in fact empirically valid) are part of the expectations (possibly subconscious) of the milieu in which the work becomes possible. The judgements made and the interpretive resources utilized in making those judgements, are not suspended in some a-social space but are part of the social practices in which conceptions of authorship develop and are consolidated.

There is a critical perspective in which the interdependence of text and reading is clearly stressed: 'the semiological understanding of language aims to show how individuals are socially constructed into reality, and how they construct that reality in the moment that it constructs them' (Ellis 1976 p.130). In the course of this book I hope to clarify the relationship between my own work and a semiotic perspective; it is sufficient for now to note that although there is clearly an important difference between semiotic analysis as unmasking the naturalness of discourse and close reading as critical exegesis, there are still good reasons for including semiotic work under the general umbrella of critical rather than constitutive analysis. The main reason is that as semiologists explore forms of discourse and types of signifying system the core of their project is to explicate 'the sign and the scientific discourse it permits': 'Semiotics is not therefore a philosophy; its domain is not that of being essence, evidence. It is basically, a theory of the processes of signifying, a *theory of knowledge* that may become either idealist or materialist according to the answer it gives to the problems of the relation matter/sense' (Kristeva 1973 p.27). The analytic project concentrates upon the sign as arbiter of sense to the relative detriment of human practice as the grounds for signification.

The thesis that a critical reading of art-work is not separate from, other than, the work itself but is rather part of that complex of expectations, attitudes and responses which constitutes the work as performance can be seen to be relevant to the debate on mass culture. Here the varying possibilities of the sense of 'mass' were crucial in promoting the relevance of different styles of inquiry. (Out of the by now vast literature on mass culture, Gans, 1974, should be mentioned as a self-conscious theorist of the varying strands, and perhaps both editions of Rosenberg and White, 1957; 1971, as sources of illustrative discussion.) Although the great majority of the participants in this debate took the issues involved very seriously it was the concern of the colonial administrator for another land. A distinction between art and popular art was taken for granted so that the critic could use the former as a kind of benchmark in order to discuss the latter, but the kinds of assumptions which made the distinction possible were not seen to be of central importance. Thus the seriousness of response was occupational rather than existential: it was 'how can we best understand these phenomena?' instead of 'how can we best live these possibilities?'. It may seem exaggerated to suggest that participation in popular art does or even can involve existential deliberation on life-prospects, but the exclusion is a cultural restriction (Tractarian narratives in the nineteenth century were more explicit about their expectations). Once it is granted that popular art can embody existential seriousness then it becomes incumbent to imbue our participation with the same seriousness. We need to ask how it is that humans express themselves in these ways and what are the implications of the manner of attempt. How performance is put together (constituted) embodies a fundamentally serious approach because it necessitates asking how can social experience, both in general and in our particular institutional context, be put together?

In trying to 'unpack' the implications of relating popular art and seriousness I have argued that our initial concerns must be with the grounds (the constitution) of shared experience. If we recognize that a constitutive approach to popular art cannot arbitrarily 'finish' at the conventional boundaries of either popularity or art, seriousness as a methodological premise can be seen as a general characteristic of a style of work — a willingness to extrapolate from the known to the unknown through a process of analogical extension. In this case the preliminary features of constitutive analysis can usefully be seen as an aspect of the more general use of the metaphor of drama in social relationships: 'I then began to perceive a form in the process of social time. This form was essentially *dramatic*. My metaphor and model here was a human aesthetic form, a product of *culture* not of nature' (Turner 1974 p.32). Turner's work has consisted of two main strands: investigation of the processual character of social dramas, the main phases of public action; and, secondly, the vocative power of ritual symbolism in dynamic developments, how they condense through reconciling normative values with physiological phenomena. Both of these strands provide analytic frames for intensive study of dramatic symbolism in social order, the increasing number of publications from Turner and his associates at Chicago shows that the approach is not restricted to tribal experience. (See also the use of Turner's conceptual formulations in the work of that sophisticated historian of popular culture Natalie Zemon Davis, 1975, especially chapters 4 and 5.) Turner's discussion of dramatism is particularly relevant to my approach because he does not take the form of his initial metaphor for granted. Although drama is necessarily structured (we cannot really say a structured occasion or performance because they imply a single event whereas cultural dramas may comprise multiple performances), the rationality of structure implies anti-structure or community. That is that there is a commitment to sociality which precedes and grounds the formal organization of social experience in any particular situation. The opposition between structure and community is not that between order and anarchy but rather that between extension and compression: 'The components of what I have called anti-structure, such as communitas and liminality, are the conditions for the production of root metaphors, conceptual archetypes, paradigms, models for, and the rest' (Turner *op. cit.* p.50). We therefore have to face the possibility that as the conditions for the production of root metaphors change, so the character of the metaphor is transformed.

One of the most powerful suggestions of a root metaphor for capitalist societies, and particularly for cultural production in such societies, has been Marx's concern with commodity relationships, the treatment of aesthetic performance as negotiable commodity. In contemporary society it may be possible to discern a new conception of aesthetic experience deriving from changes in commodity values: 'The value of such things as programmes, trips, courses, reports, articles, shows, conferences, parades, opinions, events, sights, spectacles, scenes and situations of modernity is not determined by the amount of labour required for their production. Their value is a function of the quality and quantity of *experience* they promise' (MacCannell 1976 p.23). If the character of commodities is changing in this way then there will be consequential implications for work — which will be increasingly organized in the production of leisure experiences for others. This argument leads MacCannell to his insight that tourism, as the paradigm of leisure experiences, is centrally concerned with the authenticity of social rather than individual experience: 'Although the tourist need not be consciously aware of this, the only thing he goes to see is society and its works' (*op. cit.* p.55; and thus once again the analogy between art and ethnography). The relationships we invest with significance are those in which we are able to adapt for ourselves our use of cultural resources: 'Taken together, tourist attractions and the behaviour surrounding them are, I think, one of the most complex and orderly of the several universal codes that constitute modern society, although not so complex and orderly as, for example, a language.' (*op. cit.* p.46). In order to appreciate the character and dynamism of metaphoric structures we have to go beyond the formal organization of narrative imagery and consider communication, play and fiction as communal 'bonds'. The ways these metaphors are articulated, through the dialectic of ideology and technology in highly stratified but unstable social orders is the motive for the discussion of, for example, realism and entertainment in the following chapters.

The Strategy

A curious feature of studies of popular art is recurrent insecurity about the legitimacy of the topic; thus there is usually a reference in the introduction to the criteria by which the study is justified. An example is provided by Louis Wright's pioneering study of 'middle-class culture' in Elizabethan England: he introduces his work with the observation that many of the themes he will note can be seen to be significant in the development of distinctive American cultural traditions (1935). The example is relevant because of the way it captures the functional character of justifications, the material may not be important in itself but it is relevant to more important accomplishments. I hope that these limited aspirations will be absent from this study. I have tried briefly to indicate the central role that significance and evaluation will play in the discussion of what popular art is 'about', but the values utilized are collaborative — they ask how it is that such-and-such phenomenal features (symbolic imagery) communicate — not curious sources of a mysterious entity called 'bias'. It would of course be analogous to advocating sin to declare that truth is irrelevant but I cannot pretend that I aspire to provide a truthful account of that world of events and experience which I would present as popular art. An aspiration to truth must assume the possibility of completeness, a record that is sufficient to be seen to be accurate, and I obviously cannot chart or record the phenomenal experience of every participant in popular art. I can only summarize gross features of experience as reported or hold up for discussion the ways in which experience becomes possible. The study of popular art is not necessarily about relatively unimportant characteristics of life-styles but offers a distinctive approach to social consciousness.

I should perhaps say a little more about the relationships between values and truth in the study of communication. The concept of significance assumes a relationshop to an interpretive framework, that there is not a thing which has meaning in itself but only in as much as that meaning is humanly agreed. (It may be that there are certain brute forms of signals, such as those relating to danger, which are culturally universal and operate at sub-conventional levels of response but they are so few and so conentious that they are irrelevant to the general argument.) To argue that meaning is conventional has the necessary implication that effective meaning is mediated through a series of headings such as intention, context and attention. I may claim that this prose says exactly what I mean and self-evidently so, but the reader's comprehension will obviously be facilitated by what else he knows about my character, intellectual background and political commitments etc., and thus about my probable intentions; certainly comprehension is structured by the text's publication as a book of sociology rather than as instance of another literary genre and by being published now rather than in a past or future intellectual context; and finally a hostile critic intent on displaying the errors and theoretical confusions in this work will read it considerably more closely and presumably derive more of what is 'meant' than a student reluctantly preparing for an examination. Given the variability of these and other factors it would seem to be impossible, at least unnecessary, to aim to provide a complete record of the meanings of any one 'thing', we are always concerned with meanings as they relate to specific interests. But in as much as this is true for a theorist of society contemplating a human artefact it is equally true of a naive member of society choosing popular art that he enjoys. It is for this reason that it has been a dictum of communications studies for some years that one cannot read off meaning (effect or significance) from content alone but needs to include some estimate of perceived meaning (for a fuller discussion of the relative strengths of contrasting approaches to characterizing public understanding see Chaney 1972 Part I).

I have become dissatisfied with this dictum because its adherents tend to act as though the methods of estimating perceived meaning are independent of the meaning that is being reported. Our problem here is not continually to refine methods so that it would be reasonable to hope that one day we might 'really' know what perceived meanings are, although we must recognize that such reports are always interesting and provocative. The issue is not methodological but inherent in the character of social expression. (This point does not need to be spelt out at length because it has been so forcefully articulated in the work of Kenneth Burke (1957) (see also some of the essays in Burke 1966.) The socio-historical framework within which dramatic imagery is made forceful has to interrelate with the conventions through which the imagery is read. I want to go considerably further than those of my colleagues who have wondered rather weakly whether there might not be a latent affinity between the study of cultural forms and the *verstehen* tradition in sociological inquiry. In that those who constitute the *verstehen* tradition are obviously concerned with understanding rather than describing or explaining they are sensitive to the difficulties of ascribing meanings; the approach developed in this book, however, does not assume that cultural forms are meaningful in the way that the shells of molluscs contain life — a presence to be winkled out — but tries to show that the nature of our involvement with a performance helps to constitute what that performance can mean. I hope it will be apparent that when I say a picture, for example, is meaningful I am not saying the same sort of thing as saying that it is painted in oils, i.e. a physical attribute; to say it is meaningful is to point to a world in which that meaning is possible (sensible, appropriate) and therefore the meaning is an action, it is an intervention in the orders of reality, and to understand is to collaborate. To enquire into the possibility of aesthetic force is therefore to provide some notes on forms of actions, in this case actions relating to the production and distribution of and attention to dramatic imagery.

The method used in this essay is not therefore scientific in any of the usual senses in which sociologists understand that concept. I hope the method is speculative in that it would involve gambling with what we take for granted; it is necessarily introspective in that I see no reason for assuming something to be true of others that I would discount in relation to myself (I draw a distinction here between a constitutive characteristic that might illuminate and an empirical particularity); the method is scholarly in that in preparing this work in the course of teaching and preliminary drafts I have explored without conscious bias the majority of publications either directly about or salient to popular art; it is empirical in that I start from the premise that the lived world is historically specific and therefore analysis which inquires into the grounds of that world has continually to illustrate alternatives even if these are used as points of reference rather than explored in depth; the method is critical in the sense of that word which invokes an alternative to dogmatic and/or routinized thought abstracted from the socio-political implications of social research;

and finally the method aspires to be humanistic first as part of that tradition of sociological research which has seen a commitment to the humanness of the human subject as a responsibility to consider whose side we are on, and secondly, as part of a refusal to minimize human importance compared to intellectual commitments. If a number of methodological characteristics can be summarized as an analytic stance then one could say that these features constitute a refusal to take either the warrant for the inquiry as self-evident or to take the form of knowledge as an unproblematic resource. To make yet another version of the analogy between the epistemology of popular art and the ethnographic stance, I should emphasize here that the *form* of social knowledge about popular art has to be intimately related to the perceived *forms* of that art; the essay is formalist in its self-consciousness. Although my stance may appear theoretical because it is discursive this association is not completely appropriate, in the same way that the empirical is not limited to the particular.

To the extent that there is an underlying strategy in the succeeding chapters it derives from the central issue in communication studies. This is the utility, force or even justification in drawing a distinction between medium of communication and that which is communicated. First, this issue is particularly relevant because the definitional approach advocated above of working from relations of production leads us to realize that the rapidly improving distributional facilities provided by changes in technology are essential to the populism of popular art: that widespread and impersonal accessibility through technology is the obverse of the social characteristics discussed above. It is for this reason that the literature on mass communication, and in particular its relationship to the debate on mass culture is a recurrent theme. Secondly, the relationship between medium and communication is relevant to this study in the ways in which new media require new languages. It is a truism of the culture industry that there are distinctive skills to effective expression in each medium, but the argument can be put more forcefully by saying that shifts in communication form entail a selective focusing which crucially structures the social significance of that which is communicated (relevant material recurs throughout the book but the literature is most fully discussed in the first part of the fourth chapter). Finally, and in a sense combining both of the previous aspects of the discussion of medium and message, I have tried to introduce my approach by saying it focuses on the constitution of artistic experience. I have therefore suggested that dramatic structure and social form can be importantly understood as grounds of possibility — they are the means of effective communication. It is at this level that in the concluding part the fourth chapter I try to explore some aspects of the concept of narrative form and its utility for a sociology of popular art.

In practice these analytic strategies are articulated through a structure I shall now briefly outline. After this introduction, in which basic concepts and methodological issues are outlined, in the second chapter I take up the theme of public experience. My argument is that there is a very powerful connection between our understanding of 'public' as collective experience, and 'popular' as characteristic of the collectivity. In making this connection I wish to say more than that there is a semantic overlap between the words, although the full ramifications of the connections cannot be exhaustively discussed here. I organize my discussion into three parts. The first begins with a discussion of the phenomenology of communication and the presuppositions of resources shared in common that are necessary for communication to be attempted. A concern with the ethnography of communication leads naturally to a consideration of those situations in which communication has been abstracted from a routine mode of interaction to become an ideology which provides a central metaphor for social order. In this part of the chapter I am therefore arguing that the reification of public knowledge, news as public events, serves important ideological functions. In the second part of the chapter I discuss another aspect of public order, in this case some features of the processes through which popular culture was shaped as part of the structural transformations of industrialization. Finally, in the third section the reasons for attempts to see in popular art, a way of re-thinking the relationship between art and community are introduced. As a vehicle for this discussion I use the opportunity provided by the pun in 'public place' — a physical site and a metaphoric representation of certain forms of interaction. I offer an interpretation of how some aspects of contemporary popular art have pointed to an alternative understanding of public experience.

A latent theme in the second chapter is the developing argument that popular art, in that it is centrally related to class and community consciousness, is a form of knowledge — a way of theorizing about experience. It is because the central thrust of administrative elites' hegemonic closure of discourse is to take the world of facts as an unproblematic resource — events are either shared in common or are potentially discoverable by patient research — that the initial line of resistance to this closure turns on realism as an aesthetic impulse. In the third chapter I explore some aspects of realism as an epistemological quest, as a dissatisfaction with conventional appearance that is expressed through a desire to capture 'real' features of experience. The discussion here is characteristic of the book as a whole in that I do not attempt to set out comparative styles of realism in different media, but instead, by contrasting several facets of the social contexts in which realism developed, show some of the ways in which our grasp of the real underpins conventions of appropriate fiction. The chapter is divided into the following section: the status of fictional knowledge as it is located in the process of becoming a performance — the communal recreation of experience; some reasons why reality became inherently problematic in the nineteenth century and some aspects of the ideas of Benjamin as they relate to the consequences for aesthetic representation of serial reproduction; in the next section the surrealistic juggling with conventional structures of space and time that has been characteristic of modernism in the arts and in the physical and social sciences this century is related to the preceeding discussion; finally, in the fourth section, I explore the theme of realism in the light of the general stereotype of contemporary entertainment as centrally escapist. I use the contrast between play and leisure to illustrate an argument that a distinction between types of performance is not in terms of their fidelity to a known external world but in terms of the type of reality they make possible. A culture of mass entertainment is essentially alienating because its illusions are not spectacles which facilitate questioning of reality, but reassuring, stylized versions of what we can all be assumed to 'know' already.

It will be apparent that a recurrent theme in these chapters is the 'interventionist' character of knowledge — the way knowing structures that which can be known. In relation to popular art this can be rephrased as the mode of experience structures the experience possible. To the extent that this theme is a restatement of some important ideas in cultural relativism, and particularly because the relationship between popular art and medium of communication is so intimate, in the first section of the fourth chapter I organize a discussion of the relationship between medium and message around the concept of visual literacy. My thesis here, as it is throughout the essay, is that the significance of cultural relativism turns on a prior understanding of the concept of community. Thus in the next part of the chapter I discuss some situations in which producers of art works have been more or less explicitly engaged in seeing their work as a reconstitution of community. Particular examples used here are the role of exemplary narratives in socialist societies and the 'revolutionism' of a cultural avant-garde. In the final section, the idea that fictional experience can be a constitutive metaphor for possible experience is developed through a clarification of some ideas of what is involved in a production aesthetic; the reflexive character of a concept of narrative becomes crucial here in allowing us to envisage a social theory that is not didactic but remains partisan.

2

Communication and Social Order

Authority and Dramatic Structure

I have noted the interdependence between facilities for communication and styles of popular art. I shall develop this emphasis in the course of this chapter by discussing several aspects of the social organization of 'public life' as resources for communication. To begin I have to note certain features of communication and their implications for methodology. I am concerned with how we recognize actions, be they gestural, verbal, ideographic or whatever, as potentially meaningful. The simple answer is of course that the actions are understood to be structured in terms of a 'language'; if by language we mean, as a minimum, a structured organization of rules which regularize adequate representation. Communication is therefore following a language. Although this seems clear it is not precise, we cannot be sure when our use of language as a label is straightforward or when it is analogical. For example, 'the international language of love' is an uncontentious cliché and yet we could not specify the language concerned, and other uses of language to describe interactional processes often seem to be generous. It may, therefore, be more useful to work with a concept of code. Gross has made the useful distinction between symbolic modes which are the primary frames for expression e.g. 'verbal-lexical, social-gestural and visual' etc., and a particular code which is the version of that mode available in that culture: 'A code maybe defined as an organized subset of the total range of elements, operations and ordering principles that are possible in a given mode. In the simplest sense, then, any single language is a code existing within the verbal mode. . . . Most human beings . . . need never be aware that the code they know is not co-extensive with the symbolic mode' (Gross 1973a p.192; see also 1973b). The suggestion that code and mode are equivalent for most people seems to me to be one of the more interesting dimensions of change with the development of urban-industrial cultures, in that as our social milieu becomes more fractured and heterogeneous we shift between a variety of codes both within and between symbolic modes. We may expect urban art forms not to respect code boundaries but rather to mix indiscriminately elements of codes, as in the example of popular songs.

The realization of an order to imagery does not mean that I think the signs which compose images have some inherent logic, but that order derives from human volition. When some element of the world, for example a tree, is noted in itself then we allocate the tree to an order relevant to our purposes; we may classify it as an example of a particular type of tree. When we note the same element as a sign, that is not in itself but as a representation, then we do not appropriate it to our order but interpret the sign by inferring the order through which it came to be used: thus we may see it as an indexical representation of certain qualities of 'nature'. (We may leave on one side situations, such as trees in landscaped parks, in which trees may be simultaneously available as themselves and as signs.) When we are concerned with the structured organization of signs, i.e. the language of expression, we infer that following structural conventions is intentional. To put this another way we can say that the 'orderliness' of expression does not derive from the topic but from the expressive intent of the person articulating the topic. The structure, or order, of communication is therefore the means by which sense is communicable, but the order used can only be inferred from the representational expression at hand. It is because representations are potentially meaningful: 'Communication . . . a social process within a context, in which signs are produced and transmitted, perceived and treated as messages from which meaning can be inferred' (Worth and Gross 1974 p.30), that each social process of communication involves agreement on the order to be followed. Of course this agreement is only rarely explicitly addressed, rather it is inferred from cues such as context and memories of other similar expressions and performances. We cannot get inside an author's head but we can infer the grounds through which his use of imagery is potentially meaningful by situating his work within features of a tradition or genre. The performance is the occasion for our inference of meaning, but we accumulate sense through reference to shared grounds so that performances make sense through each other.

The example of a genre as a charter which makes sense of reasonable interpretations of the intentions of producers also illustrates the provisional character of order as it is used in this discussion of communication. A recurrent use of structure, order and rules as the basis of communicative process may be read too literally. Even in speech, where the rules of grammar have been most explicitly recorded and taught to succeeding generations, everyday experience shows that adequate communication is accomplished through '*ad hoc*' rules which are convenient rather than prescriptive (see, for example, Garfinkel and Sacks 1970). Our sense of structure is therefore strategic, it is an interpretive device. This is not only true of everyday encounters, it is importantly true of that accumulation: 'The development of the word *culture* is a record of a number of important and continuing reactions to those changes in our social, economic and political life, and may be seen, in itself, as a special kind of map by means

of which the nature of the changes can be explored' (Williams 1961 p.16).
More recently Williams has returned to historical semantics as a method
for demonstrating the institutionalization of material practices in speech
forms: 'This is not a neutral review of meanings. It is an exploration of the
vocabulary of a crucial area of social and cultural discussion, which has
been inherited within precise historical and social conditions' (Williams
1976 pp. 21-2). Although the second book is more sophisticated about the
presuppositions of cultural analysis there is still a characteristic vagueness
about the 'authority' of the author which might be elucidated by turning
to another type of interpretive order, namely the presuppositions of making
a map. My remark about William's characteristic vagueness is illustrated in
his remark that 'in a number of cases, especially in certain sensitive social
and political terms, the presuppositions of orthodox opinion in that
period either show through or are *not far below the surface*' (Williams
1976 p.16 my emphasis). (A critical discussion which also notes Williams's
failure radically to query his 'authorial' stance is Eagleton 1976.)

The metaphor of map making in cultural history can be taken literally
as a way of recording the major outlines of different cultural trends.
Television programmes on art history, the organization of many museums,
coffee-table books on 'schools' are all part of the articulation of this
metaphor; so much so, that it is easy to forget the provisional character
the resulting order. Upon reflection it is not difficult to show the partial
nature of the selections which constitute such maps, it is however, more
interesting to consider the feasibility of the map-making enterprise. A part
of 'discovering' a country is to produce maps of the area, but of course,
except in very rare cases of uninhabited land, the land was not unknown
before. The inhabitants were to the map makers 'non-persons', they did
not construct their environment but were features of it. A map is a means
of reporting something 'new' to the discoverers and, more importantly,
facilitating the use of that which is discovered by those who are strangers
to it. (To use a map is to display cultural insecurity, a recognition of
distance from the milieu that is being traversed — the ubiquitous use of
models of our cultural history is a neat way of illustrating one sense of
alienation.) A shift in fictional stance involves much the same discoveries
as those in rephrasing the map: a feature of the subject is no longer 'seen
through' but now becomes the object of vision (an influential attempt to
articulate frames for vision is reported in Berger 1972). Thus it is not
coincidental that the first descriptive reports of urban working-class life-
styles were being published at the same time as 'realist' authors in the arts
were 'discovering' new subjects for fictional representation.

It is as part of a process of 're-seeing' that a map can be understood as
civilizing an alien or hostile territory, that which is unmanageable is
rendered useable, comparable. For the indigenous inhabitants the map is
likely to formulate the culture clash between insiders and outsiders
particularly starkly. The map is likely to be expressed through a series of

codes which bear little or no relation to the codification of the environment conventionally employed in indigenous practice. The idea of a scale
of distance which is independent of the means used to cross that distance,
or the idea of a set of names for physical features which do not embody
the ritual significance of those features at different points in time, both
these and many other standard map-making practices help to neutralize
an environment of its cultural density. Thus the creation of a map of some-
where 'new' to the map-maker involves recording the particular features
of that place but in ways which negate their cultural specificity – the
internal uses of the environment are at best translated, at worst obliterated,
and the whole rendered available for use. (Whether or not the social
scientist explicitly claims the ethnographic authority of the proverbial
Martian visitor, his attempts to record 'objectively' the human practices, of
his neighbours or some more exotic group, involve a related process of
neutralizing cultural density.) If I wish to respect cultural density I cannot
offer an overview of popular experience by 'describing' the major features
of contemporary entertainment. Respecting cultural specificity involves
transcending what self-evidently exists and focussing on how that specificity is articulated.

I have pointed to some of the ways in which the enterprise of making a
map, tracing a record, is an imperialistic exercise – the map maker is
formulating his version of significant detail. There is, however, a crucial
difference between a map and a narrative performance due to the fact
that one cannot go 'outside' the performance to evaluate the structure of
that performance. This is in one sense true of the representational conventions of map making, but the conventions are contingent upon certain
uses. If the map reader shares those uses and follows the conventions of
the map and does not reach the desired point, leaving reach deliberately
vague, then he can quite correctly judge the map to be inadequate. A
historical record of narrative performances shares many of the features of
a map but could not be disqualified because it did not lead you to deduce
that a particular innovation took place when it did. It is true that the
practice of art history has been as 'imperialistic' as any journey of exploration, and it is importantly true to say that we judge the adequacy of an
historical account by the coherence of the way it facilitates our reaching a
'point' be it an artist, style or movement etc. And yet a cultural history
seems even more provisional than most maps, and to be of a different
character. One reason is the vagueness of following in this context – the
examples we use are always potentially self-fulfilling prophecies: 'like
mirrors they [works of art] will reflect different facts about the age
according to the way we turn them, or the standpoint we adopt, not to
mention the tiresome tendency of mirrors to throw back our own image'
(Gombrich 1975 p.9; in thinking about these points I have been stimulated
by Gombrich's two lectures 1969 and 1975). A second reason is the
paradox that the instances we might wish to use in writing a history

provide the framework of that history: '[Michaelangelo] was famous because he was great. Whether we like or dislike him his greatness is an element in the story we are appointed to tell. It forms part of that logic of situations without which history would sink into chaos' (*op. cit.* p.55).

It is no solution to the problem posed by these reasons to retreat into a scholasticism of names and dates in which some immanent order of how it really was is brought to the surface through the use of a structure of biographical fidelity (a characteristic example which I only cite as it is a recent example of its type is Barr 1975). No solution because the biographical motif provides for the performance becoming an exemplification of life as metaphor for progress; and because the life thereby becomes a literary artefact performances exist to the extent that their description or existence can be paraphrased linguistically. In these terms an artist's life can be treated as a 'given' narrative structure. (This idea was triggered by a discussion of Panofsky in Tagg 1975; another revealing discussion of the problems posed by artists' anonymity occurs in Roskill 1976.) The utility of the biographical metaphor for cultural records may help to explain why accounts of themes in popular art, particularly Marxist accounts, have tended to replace the individual with an anthropomorphized movement or class. Another reason why scholasticism is no solution can be taken from Gombrich when he points out that a belief in facts is only possible through an implicit sense of order which legitimates the facts selected (1969 in particular pp. 14-25). The problem of what sort of record a cultural history can be is unresolvable as long as we confine ourselves to a choice between empiricism and Hegelian interconnectedness. There is a third possibility which recognizes the particularity of performances but instead of obliterating the sense which grounds performances takes the distinctive features of each as an opportunity to explore the 'form of life' within which that performance has become possible: 'He [the cultural historian] will be less interested, for example, in the economic and social causes of urban development than in the changing connotations of words such as "urbane" or "suburbia" or, conversely, in the significance of the "rustic" order in architecture' (Gombrich 1969 p.41). The connotative order of style is part of the logic of situations, but it is an order that the ethnographer, as well as the historian, participates in not observes.

The concept of connotative order is related to the study of historical semantics and in this way reminds us of a distinction that Williams emphasizes. He notes that one of the implicit functions of dictionaries is to legitimate the 'given' character of a cultural vocabulary. Thus words are given meanings and 'correct' usages 'to produce what can best be called a sacral attitude to words'. Williams wants his own work to point to an alternative approach concerned with the 'shaping and reshaping' of meanings in institutional practice. The distinction is valid and central to any aspiration to cultural description which is concerned with making meaningful rather than recording meanings. It necessarily implies, however, a recognition of ethnographic reflexivity – that our constitutive descriptions are not parallel to but embedded in the meanings they 'report', that 'what we call our data are really our own constructions of other people's constructions of what they and their compatriots are up to' (Geertz 1973 p.9). The study of communicative practices is therefore continually engaged with the validity of abstraction, in the sense of abstracting a text (performance) to be interpreted. This is not to say that all communicative practices ranging from interpersonal speech through map making, narrative fictions and ritual symbolism constitute equivalent texts, but that reading presumes an ability to recognize 'something' to read, boundaries to performance, as well as an ability to read: 'Doing ethnography is like trying to read (in the sense of 'construct a reading of') a manuscript – foreign, faded, full of ellipses, incoherencies, suspicious emendations, and tendentious commentaries, but written not in conventionalized graphs of sound but in transient examples of shaped behaviour' (*op. cit.* p.10). At this stage it becomes appropriate to devote some attention to an alternative strategy to the dominant analytic style of this essay. The alternative has been particularly relevant throughout this section in that I have emphasized the salience of concepts of code, rules and conventions for reading as presuppositions for communicative process. I refer to the alternative strategies available in the structuralist tradition; precisely because it is not 'a' strategy and because this is not an essay about structuralism I shall only choose one example to illustrate differences between structuralism and my approach.

The example I shall use is a secondary source, and therefore suffers all the faults of 'explaining' a strategy to novitiates, but it has the advantage of unusual clarity. Culler (1975) begins his introduction to the study of poetics by pointing to the crucial importance of literary conventions in framing distinctions between types of performance. He makes the sensible point that a 'poem' is a puzzling, and frequently incoherent, collage of words until one knows it is a poem and it then acquires a literary rather than a grammatical structure. This is why he makes a distinction between being able to translate and being able to understand a poem, between knowing what something means and understanding its meaning. Thus I could replace all the words of a poem with appropriate words from another language but the second set of words would not display a grasp of the fictional logic, the sense of the original set. Culler's explanation of this is that knowing literary conventions requires a process of learning much as knowing the conventions of a language such as English requires learning. These uncontroversial arguments provide a basis for more controversial propositions. He argues that the common underpinning role of conventions in both literary and verbal discourse means that a grasp of such conventions is a presupposition for understanding in either or both modes. 'Grasp' is a competence which readers (speaker-hearers) must possess in order to employ the conventions to read; and therefore a study of literary

experience should not be deflected into recording unique features of
particular works or the motives of particular authors, but should explore
the conventions through which works become potentially meaningful:
'Study of the linguistic system becomes theoretically coherent when we
cease thinking that our goal is to specify the properties of objects in a
corpus and concentrate instead on the task of formulating the internalized
competence which enables objects to have the properties they do for
those who have mastered the system' (Culler 1975 p.120).

Culler argues that in order to study the grounds of fictional experience
we need a theory of the rules of reading, the institutionalized modes of
articulating fictional competence in different cultural contexts. The difference between his strategy and the one argued in this book is that
Culler's approach is not a theory of 'reading' as one might normally
understand the word, but a concern with the ability to read which must
underlie literary discourse: 'The conventions of poetry, the logic of
symbols, the operations for the production of poetic effects, are not
simply the property of readers but the basis of literary forms' (*op. cit.*
p.117). Therefore 'discourse' in this approach is not something constituted
by the practice of reading (speaking) but a potential inherent in texts
(performances): 'The goal of all structuralist activity, whether reflexive
or poetic, is to reconstruct an "object" in such a way as to manifest thereby the rules of functioning (the "functions") of this object', 'Structuralism,
in particular, can be defined historically as the passage from symbolic
consciousness to paradigmatic consciousness' (Barthes 1972 pp.214,206).
It may by now be clear why the structuralist strategy is particularly
attractive to those critics who aspire to impersonal interpretation, there
is an aura of objectivity, a 'science' of possible reading rather than the
subjectivity of evaluation thus it seems to justify an analysis of ideologies
which transcends ideology. How any particular reader interprets, mis-
interprets, a text can be dismissed as the vagaries of performance — *what
is of interest are the readings the text facilitates*. The concern is with the
possibilities of the text rather than the constitutive practices of reading.

The key to my objection to this strategy is the hypostatization of
discourse that structuralism entails. Theories which stress a concept of
competence as a prerequisite for comprehensibility characterize communication as the exercise of individual faculties rather than as the social
negotiation of interaction. Discussing the relevance of Chomsky's theories
of grammatical competence to studies of communicative comprehensibility Hymes draws a distinction between short-term innate competence to
acquire particular language skills and long-term social competence to
negotiate a biography of cultural environments. Hymes argues that
Chomsky's distinction between acceptable and grammatical, with strong
emphasis upon the latter, must be superseded in favour of a fourfold
distinction: whether something is in fact done (and what its doing entails).
If material relevant to these distinctions is pursued a broad theory of

competence will emerge which combines a much wider range of material:
'*In sum, the goal of a broad theory of competence can be said to show the
ways in which the systematically possible, the feasible, and the appropriate
are linked to produce and interpret actually occuring cultural behaviour*'
(Hymes 1972, p.286, emphasis in original). I do not deny the significance
of structuralist work but I wish to show why, despite a common concern
with constitutive practices, I am pursuing a very different strategy.
Because I am concerned with fictional experience, because: 'the conclusion that knowing how to wink is winking and knowing how to steal a
sheep is sheep-raiding is to betray as deep a confusion as . . . to identify
winking with eyelid contractions or sheep raiding with chasing woolly
animals out of pastures' (Geertz *op. cit.* p.12), I am concerned with
fictional discourse as it is 'broadly' accomplished, with the necessity of
attempting a 'thick' description. Bending Geertz to the argument of this
section I can say that such description is not a recording (a mirror or a
photograph), but an inscription. It constitutes an account which aspires to
adequacy and fidelity: 'The essential task of theory building here is not to
codify abstract regularities . . . not to generalize across cases but to
generalize within them' (*op. cit.* p.26).

Popular narratives are descriptions of social experience and therefore
their authors have to draw upon often implicit agreements about how we
accomplish collective life, by generalizing within instances. Urban society
is structured by barriers for privacy where the masks of public identity
can be suspended or transformed into a different set of more private
habits and activities. The characteristic themes of popular narratives are
concerned with the overlap of these areas of social expectations, with the
tensions that derive from dissonant roles or from the excitement of
fantastic opportunities to escape the restrictions of conventional roles.
One way of understanding what is going on in popular fiction is to look
at different types of story-telling as different ways of thinking about what
the collectivity we share is. In other words what are the implications of
discussing social experience for the nature of the experience that is being
discussed, the reflexivity of self-consciousness. In the remainder of this
section I shall develop this theme by a consideration of the dramatization
of facts necessary for the production of 'public' events called news. I shall
begin by discussing Gouldner's book on the 'origins, grammar and future
of ideology', in which he addresses the two consequences of pursuing the
staging (dramatization) of collective experience: what are the sources of
change in the character of political publics? And to what extent is social
theory inherently ideological? One reason why Gouldner's book is apposite
is that he not only accepts that changes in the means of public communication constitute a communications revolution, but argues that this
revolution underlies irreversible shifts in the drama of public experience.

The first point to be made is that ideology, modernity and the development of political publics are interdependent. Modernity is to be

understood as bourgeois venality or rationality, it is a situation in which the world of mutual experience is accepted as a more or less convenient construct held together by tactical considerations. 'The specific socio-cultural conditions under which the modern grammar of rationality matures is: the waning of once traditional cultures; the decline in the sheer givenness of its values; the corresponding increased visibility of the rules that had hitherto largely remained unnoticed; the rise of cities and/or urbanism, the rise of new social classes, the decline of older established elites, and the intensifying struggles among them; increasing travel, commerce, improved modes of communication and transportation, bringing increased *confrontation* among different cultures and within their bearers' (Gouldner 1976 p.50). Within these changes ideology is the 'self-consciousness of ordinary language', it is the way in which individuals can handle the discrepancy between surface and meaning — a rhetoric which could mobilize the word as rationale for deeds. Gouldner's thesis is therefore that the Hobbesian world of bourgeois consciousness is only possible when the breakdown of traditional communities undercuts the stability of 'established facts'; within such a world ideologies are rational discourse because they are persuasive rather than authoritative; and that therefore new communities based on worlds of discourse develop, these are publics ('non-traditional structures') made up by their means of communication: 'Historically speaking, then, a 'public' consists of people who habitually acquire their news and orientations from impersonal mass media (*op. cit.* p.96). The interdependence of publics and ideologies is that both are constituted by their manner of discourse: 'Ideologies, then, may be further defined as symbol systems generated by, and intelligible to, persons whose relationship to everyday life is mediated by their reading — of newspapers, journals and books — and by the developing general concept of "news" ' (*op. cit.* p.105).

The second point derives straightforwardly from the first. This is that the consciousness of inhabitants of post-traditional social experience is centrally structured by developments in means of public communication. One way in which this claim might be interpreted is not particularly controversial, this is that the mass media decentralize knowledge. By this one means that there is a democratization of ideas, the media are a public facility to which all have an ostensible right of access. At the time of technological innovation the democratic plurality of ideas is often complemented by the physical plurality of points of production, as with the proliferation of printing presses in the seventeenth century, but the physical plant is usually subsequently constrained and centralized. The more controversial interpretation is that democratization leads to a climate of rationality, controversial because so many features of industrial society seem so outrageously irrational, but here rationality is used as 'self-groundedness' — 'that the speaker be able to state articulately all the premises required by his argument.' Post-traditional consciousness is in

these senses democratic and rational but precisely because of these qualities
it is abstracted: 'The *dialogue* character of discourse thus tends to become
occluded, as focal attention is given over to the printed object or to its
words or ideas . . . . It is now easier to assume that the *meaning* of a communication (as distinct from its *validity*) may be understood apart from
the intent and occasion of the speech and the speaker' (*op. cit.* pp. 43-4).
These changes in consciousness may be summarized as the development of
the possibility of a distinction between public opinion and private view.
(As an aside I will note that this analysis is not only possible in retrospect,
in a book originally published in 1828 McKinnon (1971) discusses the
development of public opinion as it is correlated with the rise of the
middle classes.)

The first two points that we can take from Gouldner are that the
transition to modernity was essentially constituted by the central role
of impersonal mass media, and that the means of transition was a distinction between public consciousness and private opinion. The third point
derives directly from its predecessors and concerns the contradictions in
the concept of public in media-based democracies. I have suggested that
the interdependence of publics and ideologies is in their shared manner of
discourse — a concern with a realm of public events, and in order to be
effective both aspire to a rationality of accessible premises; that is that
there be no ascribed restrictions on knowledge and discourse. The contradiction is that if public events are 'open' as rationality demands, they are
unstable and splinter: 'The central problem of the new society therefore
concerned its *public* sphere and especially its political institutions; . . .
Political issues came to centre on the kinds of social structures that might
provide continuity and stability in a public sphere where family-transmis-
sable privilege was no longer accepted,' (*op. cit.* pp. 198-9). This instability
was inherent because if there are no *a priori* sources of authority then
'convincing accounts of social reality may now issue from different
quarters' so that 'definitions of reality become pluralized'. The legitimacy
of the state has continually to be demonstrated and in particular the
domination of state power by stable elites has to be justified if it cannot
be masked. There is therefore an intimate connection between the
organization of public communication and the significance of censorship
in media-based democracies. . . In capitalist societies the question of
censorship has usually been phrased in terms of restrictions on mercantile
capitalism, restraints on business access to a market, and could thus be
presented as an ethical issue in contrast to the situation in state-centralist
societies where censorship is more overtly the formulation of official
reality. To confine censorship to a problem of controlling the distribution
of commodities is, however, to ignore the more fundamental issue of
competence: 'the manner in which the structure of communication allows
some issues to be seen and spoken, while inhibiting and diverting attention
from still others.' (*op. cit.* p.146). The contradiction in the concept of

public is therefore an inherent struggle by different groups in the hierarchy of social order over 'gaps between accounts of social reality fostered by the managers, owners and leaders of the society' and the understanding of social experience possible to the managed.

I hope it will be apparent that my reading of Gouldner is not exhaustive but has been organized to bring out the relevance of his approach to my argument. It seems to me that Gouldner is arguing that ideological consciousness requires the rationality of public discourse but that in an hierarchically stratified society this rationality is constrained and distorted by a conception of collectivity as dependent. In my terms the public sphere is a dramatic concept in which the possible meanings of perform-ances are limited by the structure of social relationships through which the performances are distributed. If I can take it back to an initial dialectic: the meaning of performances is ostensibly a multitude of reports of the world as it is; but it can be argued that the structure of public discourse (the organization of competence), that is the hegemonic impulse to restrict reports to those consonant with official conceptions of reality, makes the ostensible meaning meaningless; and thus we have to find a way of characterizing apparent meaninglessness — the dialectic is in a continual tension between meaning and form. To this point I have tried to show how a metaphor of society as drama can be used to illuminate relationships of production in public communication. The next step is to look at some of the literature on the production of news in contemporary public dis-course, with particular reference to the conceptions of public as commu-nity which underlies and makes sensible news-gathering activities.

In one sense the authors or producers of fictional performances for mass communication, be they books, plays or films etc., intend their work much as any other creative author; the problem is that a large part of the material available through mass media is not explicitly authored and thereby authorized as fictional but is presented as facts or news about the world. For this latter work the author or reporter is ideally neutral or even invisible — his work is not intended by him but is somehow 'caused' by the way the world is. We can get some sense of the significance of this point by considering the analogous situation of factual reports within a traditional communal environment. If A reports something to B within such a community, whether it is a matter for alarm or rejoicing or what-ever, he is thereby claiming a familiarity with the judgements of relevance currently shared in the community such that it would be generally agreed that this is a matter worthy of report. A's warrant for the report is presumably, besides the intrinsic interest of the events reported, to display his membership of the community and, by giving another example, to reinforce the conventions that make this event reportable. He intends by his report to set his news within what he presumes to be the consensus over things that 'matter' to the community. The news reporter working within the organizational framework of a communications industry is drawing on the logic of this situation to provide a warrant of intentionality for his reports: 'The journalistic attitude is evoked by the needs for the periodistic presentation of images of the world to distant publics who are not able to comprehend necessary parts of their world in terms of their direct experience' (Bensman and Lilienfeld 1973 p.148). His work can only communicate by presuming some meta-community, possibly global, which provides conventions for news-worthiness to be relied upon in discriminating between those features of the world to be reported and those to be ignored. Not only is reality not self-evident, much of the reporter's skill rests in judicious juggling of distinctions between appearance and reality: 'journalism not only reports on the operation of appearances, and on realities underlying appearances, but also creates appearances or the appearance of realities' (*op. cit.* p.136).

One reason why newsmen are suspicious of sociological interpretations of their work may be that newsmen are suspicious of theorizing in general. The conventions of routine news-gathering are likely to be organizationally effective and to be reassuring by resolving practical problems of what 'sort of thing' a particular item of news is: 'The more widely the old conventions are shared . . . the greater the consensus in the journalistic community on what news should be: and the more they publish the same information the more assured they feel about the validity of that information' (Sigal 1973 p.74). Some relevant illustrative material is reported in the paper by Tuchman on the ways in which newsmen's work pre-judges the significance of the content of their reports. The conventional response of the profession to queries concerned with the allocation of resources is to differentiate categories of news. The problem with any list of categories, as a governing catalogue authorizing resource allocation, is that they can only be prototypes to which particular events-as-news have to be allocated. Thus the distinction between hard news and soft news in terms of importance versus interest is in practice only provisional and events slip between categories on other grounds. Tuchman (1973 p.117) suggests it is more useful to see newsmen's classifications as typifications 'in which the relevant characteristics are central to the solution of practical tasks or problems at hand and are constituted in and grounded in everyday activity'. The importance of this shift in labelling is that it directs our attention to how newsmen control their resources. There is always too much news and too much work to be done, so that there are inherent choices about type and degree of response to events, choices which crucially determine the ways in which those events become news: 'The construction of reality through redefinition, reconsideration, and reaccounting is an ongoing process. The newsmen's typifications indicate that it might be valuable to think not as distorting, but rather as reconstituting the everyday world' (*op. cit.* p.129).

The more general implication of studies of news making for themes of this chapter is that the social organization of production of public communication can be seen to be providing the frame of communal consensus necessary for ordering significance of events. I have argued above that the dissemination of news as 'the way the world is' (*vide* Walter Cronkite) depends upon an implicit sense of a meta-community in which the world is unproblematic; we can now be more specific and say that the 'patterned and perceptually shared past, present and future' which is community history, i.e. 'the world', is indexed in the sense of is shown through public events: 'Thus the content of an individual's conceptions of the history and the future of his or her collectivity comes to depend on the processes by which public events get constructed as resources for discourse in public matters' (Molotch and Lester 1974 pp.102-3).

If we approach the relationship between news and democratic discourse in terms of a conceptual model of distinct 'publics' and 'events', the two realms to be linked by media of communication, then a vocabulary of public demands and needs becomes appropriate. This is very much the model of communication articulated by employees and other defendants of the contemporary organization of public communication in their rare moods of theoretical reflection. One can see here the way in which the presumption of a legitimating meta-community is taken to be non-problematic, then the existence of that community as audience, like a voracious child, can be pointed to in explanation of programming policies: as the media are merely channels for reporting the way the world is, their performances are responses to public taste. The alternative being developed here is that the public is not independent of its activities and therefore the ways in which those activities 'will have turned out to be' constitutes the possibilities for public experience. Thus although realities are not more or less true they are strategic in that public experience is shaped in ways that are functional for the maintenance of an hierarchical social order: 'For the citizen to read the newspaper as a catalogue of the most important happenings of the day, or for the social scientist to use the newspaper for uncritically selecting topics of study, is to accept as reality the political work by which events are constituted by those who happen to currently hold power' (Molotch and Lester *op. cit.* p.111).

The argument can now be phrased more broadly, the presumption of a meta-community which provides a frame of legitimation for the media of public communication is not just a convenient fiction — it provides a groundwork of meaning for public events in ways that are inimical to communal self-reflection. To put it more simply, one can say that the naive view of public communication is of a mirror held up to society, or of a telescope which focuses public attention with fidelity. Both metaphors imply that the meaning of events is inherent in the events and the process of communication makes this meaning available. This view is naive because any collectivity is an organization of relationships of power, and the meaning of events is contextual and shifts in relation to the aspirations and intentions of participants. The plurality of sense in a heterogeneous society can be recognized and can be used as an opportunity for public communication, in Brecht's phrase, to 'give a truly public character to public occasions'; in practice our talk about ourselves has usually served to legitimate the *status quo* and inhibit communal consciousness. For example, one can point to studies of the reporting of demonstrations and political conflict in general and industrial conflict in particular, the development of 'moral panics' in relation to 'crime waves', the dismissive response to changing sexual relationships and the stereotyping of racial minorities. The general implication of these studies is that the producers of public communication have been able to present their version of consensus as the middle ground, the self-evident point of neutrality which does not need to be advocated. A professionalism of communication which ensures that there is nothing to be communicated (*cf.* Elliott 1973 chap. 8).

I have been arguing that the organization and distribution of performances for public communication has presumed an unproblematic intelligibility for its resources and thus an ideology of professional neutrality. This ideology is functional for the social order in two ways: it, first, serves to disguise the contentious character of the 'reality' that is being reported; and secondly, it attempts to provide a frame for public experience as that experience which can be typified. An instance of this process comes in a report of a study of media coverage of the 1974 US Congressional elections, the author noted that the use of the media in their campaign by the candidates had become one of the topics for the media; so that instead of simply reporting endorsement X by a candidate the media report his endorsement in the context of what the media understands the candidate's strategy to be — with the paradoxical consequence that candidates get better coverage if they can provide a comprehensible strategy for the media to use in interpreting their policies, i.e. if they can convince the media of the sophistication of their 'meta-campaign' (Carey 1976). Thus we find many examples of outraged minorities resorting to disruption as the only way they can break the vicious circle that it is the powerful who make news. Examples one might cite are student sit-ins and sudden and intransigent strikes, or even inter-racial strife in Southern Africa. The characteristic treatment of these disruptions, however, is not as events-in-themselves but as instances of disruptive activity. The events are reported as problems to be solved in order to ensure the maintenance of the social order, and it is a small step from this starting point to attempt to 'explain' dissidence in terms of a failure to realize the prior needs of the social order. Workers would not be disruptive if they realized there was a higher interest above their sectional concerns, and a failure to 'realize' must mean there has been a failure of communication. The circle has now been closed and we can see that some of the reasons why public communication is so frequently held to be crucial to contemporary industrial societies. The world of public

events assumes an over-arching community of which we are all members,
the salience of this community is continually displayed through assembling and reporting experience, and therefore any failures in recognizing
the responsibilities of membership must be due to inadequacies in communication. From familial quarrels, through disputes in firms, schools and
colleges, and even including socio-economic class conflict it is possible
and frequently attempted to locate the source of tension in deficiencies
of communication (an interesting discussion of some of the ways communication has been reified as an 'explanation' of social problems comes
in Hall and Hewitt 1970). The presumption of shared communal interests
which makes such a diagnosis possible is yet another instance of social
analysis in which the collectivity is taken as something accomplished to
be preserved, rather than as an accumulating reality, a set of practices, to
be created, maintained and transformed.

The ways in which we have been discussing the communal articulation
through modes of communication should help to make clearer the argument that the conceptualization of public as audience in the production
of mass communication has inhibited popular collective consciousness. It
may be objected that the illustrative material I have touched upon has
been concentrated upon resources for public debate. I do not believe this
was forced upon me and in the next part of the chapter I discuss some
features of the development of popular entertainment and the implications
of this history for communal consciousness. My concern in these sections
is to explore the dramatic scenarios in popular culture for the modes of
experience they make possible. The interactionist position with its stress
on meaningful implications of experience to actors, provides a basis for
us to point to the deficiencies of causal imagery and as such has underlain
a revival of interest in communication as negotiation. My dissatisfaction
is not that this approach is wrong but that it leaves our inquiry at the
level of asking 'what is going on inside the heads of members of this
audience?' Thus the naive cocktail question 'what can somebody get out
of (for example) pornography?' only allows answers in terms of deviant
interests (if we robustly say with Susan Sontag 'stimulation' — we stop
the conversation); the alternative inverts the direction of the question —
'why is it that this is thought pornographic?' — and asks about that which
makes the topic possible. In so doing we do not outlaw moral categories
but ask more closely about what can be accomplished within differing
moral perspectives. That is we shift from asking about the insides of heads
to what could meanings mean.

Popular Culture and Social Control

In chapter 1 I attempted to set out the initial features of my approach
to the study of popular art. In the course of outlining a methodology
based on productive relationships I distinguished conventional features of

the production of popular as opposed to that art conventionally known as 'high', serious or academic. Briefly, these were that academic art is oriented towards canons of individualism, accords with official norms of seriousness, and celebrates inspirational production while popular art is collectively manufactured to appeal to unofficial tastes. When making these points I explicitly suspended discussion of the distinctions between folk art and popular culture, because it seems to me that in making these distinctions we become involved in a more wide-ranging discussion of cultural change and social control. More explicitly, material relating to the emergence of popular art as urban experience is necessarily focused upon the transfiguration of norms of folk culture as a crucial part of a process of cultural stripping and re-socialization: the fashioning of a labour force appropriate to the changing context of relations of production. To the extent that the difference between folk and popular is an index of a revolutionized social order, the administrative control of performances will be one way in which the politics of a changing social structure will be articulated.

In order to elucidate this theme I shall briefly survey some salient features of fictional experience in folk socities. Although I do not wish to seem to be endorsing 'an unsophisticated acceptance' of 'a pure folk at one end of the continuum and Volkswagens at the other end' (Moss 1971 p.58), I think it appropriate to use an ideal-typical characterization of art-work in folk societies to ground my analysis of the implications or urban-industrialization for popular culture. If only because we need to bring out some crucial shifts in the nature of 'performance' between folk and popular experience. Given that expressive symbolism, at whatever level of complexity or sophistication, is a universal feature of folk culture, it is legitimate to ask if there are common features to the modes of production and performance of such symbolism. Without claiming that each of these features will necessarily be present in relation to any particular item of expressive symbolism, I believe it will be useful to mention four common features: such symbolism is characteristically performed; it is organic; it totalizes meaning; and it articulates structural order.

In expanding these headings we note that such symbolism is a perform-ance rather than a commodity, that is that the symbols are utilized as part of a 'happening' — they are physically enacted. Even when this is not the case the symbolic embellishment of material objects is designed to form part of such a ceremonial; more generally one can say that the symbolism is only sensible when located in ceremonial context. Another way of putting this is that the symbolism tends to be valueless to the members of the relevant society, it has significance through its use not as an object in its own right. Closely linked with this feature is the second that such symbolism is organic in the sense that it is organized around a 'natural' time-scale; either the progress of the seasons or the social organization of 'biological' events such as maturity, marriage and reproduction. The interdependence of the community with the progress of seasonal time gives a collective character to performances — they are likely to be communal celebrations. And as such frequently involve the suspension of conventional social order, they become licensed occasions for suspending rules of sexual propriety or involve structural inversion such that the usually powerful are forced for a limited period to be humbled by their inferiors. Although one can point to specific functions for the wide range of expressive performances, their collective character points to a third feature which I have called totalizing meaning. By this I mean that there is a shared latent function to such performances which is to reaffirm the communal way of life. Traditional forms are not just obligations but to recognize their binding force is to admit a community in which they have force, and therefore there is a layer of meaning to folk art which is fundamentally sacral — although the activities involved may appear rigorously secular. The idea of latent meaning leads to my fourth feature which is that the composite elements in the symbolism of the performance are structurally ordered such that they can be analysed in terms of a cognitive order which no individual member of that community may be able to report or even comprehend.

The characterization of folk experience that has been given so far is meant to be paradigmatic, in practice the decay of village culture was necessarily protracted and involved an enormous degree of overlap and a gradual changing of dominant tone and style: 'It seems to me that there are a number of respects in which the agrarian life of medieval Western Europe continued to display some of these more primitive features. . . . such as the lack of . . . clearly defined periods of leisure as such, but economic activities, like hunting or market-going, obviously have their recreational aspects, as do singing or telling stories at work' (Thomas 1964 p.52). It is sufficient for our purposes to note that much of the force of the contrast between folk and popular is captured by the significance of towns in medieval lore and experience. To the extent that the countryside was populated by reasonably stable communities the pattern of expressive life was organic in the sense discussed above. Festivals and other ceremonialized occasions, as well as more spontaneous narratives, songs and pastimes, were cast in traditional moulds and characteristically performed by amateurs, that is local inhabitants who did not derive their sole source of income from performing. This fabric of shared collective pastimes was shot through with elements derived from or provided by the more professional skills or urban entertainment (although one must not exaggerate the dichotomy, urban life was patterned, ritualized, collective and local in ways inconceivable to metropolitan inhabitants; see Lofland's interesting discussion of pre-industrial and early industrial cities (1973)). Obviously the degree of urban influence would vary with factors such as proximity, accessibility, mechanization of objects and pictures (*cf.* the role of pedlars) in particular the development of printing, and its implications for the development of a shared vernacular form (see N.Z. Davis's (1975 esp. chap.7)) discussion of the interaction of literate and oral culture. To summarize, it seems reasonable to think of a period stretching over several centuries in which the cultural life of the people was predominantly local and communal, although there were always particular variations in the degree to which this experience was supplemented by forms of commercial entertainment. It is for this reason, doubtless, that the literature on pre-industrial popular culture often employs the concepts of folk and popular interchangeably.

I have suggested that the character of urban culture was an important influence on the degree and types of commercialization of popular leisure. Although my remarks on the characteristics of the transitions from folk to popular are very preliminary, if we note two other areas of significant influence it may help to illustrate succeeding arguments. They are the status of festivals and crowds as examples of collective life, and some features of popular narratives. The significance of crowd or mob gatherings and actions as forms of public life recurs throughout this part of the chapter. The starting-point for raising the topic at this stage is Rudé's thesis that crowds are historical phenomena which differ in character and structure as societies change. The pre-industrial crowds of eighteenth-century Paris and London changed as 'predominant traditional and "indigenous" beliefs . . . were gradually rivalled or eclipsed by the new political ideas emanating from the French Revolution and the working-class movements of the 1830s and 1840' (Rudé 1971 p.33). Rudé is centrally concerned with movements of popular protest but the imagery and rhetoric in which such explosions of feeling were couched was drawn from festive forms and other traditions of social classification (in developing this theme I am indebted to Natalie Davis 1975). The carnival as a seasonal celebration also provided an opportunity for moral satire of deviance and a functional institution for village adolescents. When such carnivals were staged in the more complex contexts of urban life the form evolved and became ambiguously caught up with more abstract elements of political and social criticism: 'The urban Abbeys of Misrule lost much of their vitality by the eighteenth century, but along the way they had called members of the lower order to noise their political complaints. Indeed, charivaris of a political nature are found in a city and countryside into the nineteenth century' (Davis *op. cit.* p.123; although Professor Davis brings this out in her text it is important to note here the interaction between the playful exploration of order and constraint in festivals and the metaphoric significance of games in literature best explored by Bakhtin, 1969). The idea of public drama as secular morality plays such as carnivals which are independent of conventional theatrical settings does not die out in contemporary society but is significantly transformed (see Grimes 1976).

The last illustrative area for the transition from folk experience to more popular forms I wish to describe briefly is that of popular narratives. We might think that the contrast between folk and popular can be precisely captured here by a distinction such as that between oral and literate culture. In practice, however, the same difficulties recur: 'The basic point then, is the continuity of "oral" and "written" literature. There is no deep gulf between the two: they shade into each other both in the present and over many centuries of historical development . . . The idea of pure and uncontaminated "oral culture" as the primary reference point for the discussion of oral poetry is a myth' (Finnegan 1976 p.24). Although histories of street literature are interesting in this context (See Neuberg 1976; Collison 1973; Shepard 1973), I have decided to note a couple of points from Kunzle's (1973) history of narrative strips and picture stories. The contemporary term 'popular imagery' is a heterogeneous category ' . . . for any kind of cheap printed picture destined for the less-educated classes: representations of saints, madonnas, folk heroes, monsters, natural miracles, domestic animals, toy soldiers, playing cards, illustrations to ballads and folk plays' (Kunzle 1973 p.4). Given the nature of this category it is not surprising that the oldest survivals of narrative strips are dominated by religious themes, although the most common moral is the necessity to obey the Ten Commandments and/or to avoid the seven deadly sins. The folk character of this moral didacticism is brought out by the use of crude metaphors of cartography and travel to structure narratives of moral pitfalls and the temptations of vice. Similarly the most common sin was seen to be gluttony 'which in the broadsheet illustrations was rendered in a map dotted with landscape features such as the tree laden with hams, the lake filled with milk and honey etc., — and human figures engaged in appropriate activities' (*op. cit.* p.216). However, these 'folk' characteristics can be exaggerated because, as the original definition indicated, popular imagery in the sense used here is dependent upon printing and in the first centuries of its development is concentrated in urban centres and dominated by themes of political and religious propoganda. Thus it becomes more explicable that an early master of comic imagery, Durer's follower Hans Sebald Beham, used his 'considerable flair for depicting rustic life' cruelly to satirize rural brutishness because 'one should remember that peasant customs in early sixteenth-century Germany were not, for the burgher, merely harmless matters for humorous observation; they gained, in the light of terrible peasant revolts, particular topical urgency' (*op. cit.* p.28). To avoid the recurrent problems of attempting to classify 'break-points' between folk and popular concerns, it may be easier to adopt McCormack's (1969) suggestion that we substitute amateur and applied for folk and popular respectively. We could then say that as the majority of the population becomes urbanized the areas for amateur expression were increasingly constrained and privatized.

My argument is that during the long transition from medieval to industrial society, folk and popular as cultural categories overlapped because both were forms of life. In order to elucidate the sense in which form of life is being used in this context I propose briefly to discuss E.P. Thompson's (1971) paper on the 'moral economy' of the eighteenth-century English crowd. Thompson is concerned to argue against the 'pathological' view of food riots in the eighteenth century, that is that they were spasmodic convulsions of desperate men. Against this view he argues for the salience of legitimating notions in justifying disruptive actions: 'By the notion of legitimation I mean that the men and women in the crowd were informed by the belief that they were defending traditional rights and customs; and, in general, that they were supported by the wider consensus of the community' (*op. cit.* p.78). The grounds of legitimacy are held to lie in a 'moral economy' — 'a consistent traditional view of social norms and obligations' — which, if we are to understand the moral assumptions of this traditional view, we must conceive 'that there may have been a time, within a smaller and more integrated community, when it appeared to be "unnatural" that any man should profit from the necessities of others, and when it was assumed that, in time of dearth, prices of "necessities" should remain at a customary level, even though there might be less all round' (*op. cit.* pp.131-2). It may be difficult for us to grasp these moral assumptions because by the end of the eighteenth century they had been superseded by an alternative social configuration in which the public is an anomic collection of self-seeking individuals, a political economy appropriate to the rationality of industrial capitalism. The 'traditional' modes of social protest did not disappear overnight and traces lingered well into the nineteenth century, but the fears of Jacobinism at the end of the previous century allied with the shortages produced by the war grounded a more explicit version of social conflict. 'The forms of action which we have been examining depended upon a particular set of social relations, a particular equilibrium between paternalist authority and the crowd' (*op. cit.* p.129), such an equilibrium was both unnecessary and untenable in the climate of individualist rationality promoted through political economy.

It is because the emergent rationality found local customs and commitments inappropriate encumbrances that such a web of affiliations, festivals and entertainments had to be supplemented by a more abstract political community. It is possible to see that if national politics was to have the role of articulating public consciousness the representativeness of the public forum becomes an important topic; and thus the debates on the reform of political institutions become part of broader processes of social change. These processes I shall characterize as centrifugal — a climate in which the power of local customs was condemned as irrational to be supplanted by sensible, coherent policies emanating from an administrative elite. In relation to popular culture the climate of centrifugalism was supplemented and reinforced by a concern for the preservation of structural stability allied with perceived opportunities for commercial profit; so that there were national administrative pressures on cultural forms to facilitate what relevant elites could agree to be tolerable diversity within implicit consensus. In the remainder of this section I shall discuss four modes of incorporation, or types of pressure, which acted to structure the cultural politics of the emergent society. These modes are: commercialization, supplanting amateur production of perfrmances by commercially-inspired professionals; suppression, deliberate attempts to stamp out or control what were felt to be illegitimate performances; bourgeoisification, a process in which a concern for respectability came to supplant the value of vitality; and alienation, the transformation of the experience of work so that for the majority it becomes alienating with consequential implications for leisure. Although I shall discuss these modes separately they are conceived interdependently and their significance derives from elements shared in common. I should also say that although these pressures were more or less understood by contemporaries, this does not mean that they were completely inspired by conscious self-seeking. Cultural change, like all other forms of social change, is only susceptible to identifiable will.

It seems to be a recurrent feature of studies of popular culture that they are written as mourning the passing of relics of folk culture. For example, in one of the collections of ethnographic reports by Mass Observation there is a study of totems in a Wakes week in a Lancashire town ('A Slight Case of Totemism' in Madge and Harrisson 1939). Such survivals are interesting because they point to those aspects of tradition which are most resistant to commercialization. In Dorson's (1971) discussion of cultural traditions which survive migration to new urban contexts he mentions ethnic churches as folk institutions and in particular the manner of celebrating the feast days of such churches. The 'sacred' character of such institutions should help to preserve them from deliberate exploitation although feast-type occasions always run the risk of being noticed as quaint survivals and being turned into spectacles for casual tourists. There is inevitably a thin dividing line between a festival preserved because of its living significance in the lives of participants and one designed as a set of routines colourfully staged for onlookers. To appreciate that the line is being crossed may necessitate being sensitive to a process of stylization which is a concomitant of the transition from festival to spectacle. Other cultural traditions Dorson mentions are ethnic cuisine and oral narratives particularly those associated with personal histories. An interesting aspect of the latter point is the interest shown by some folklorists in the uses to which families put relatively recent resources such as that provided by a collection of photographs in constituting a domestic biography.

Bearing these points in mind it is absurd to deny any persistence of folk traditions in urban society, but research in industrial folklore has really to escape a straitjacket of nostalgia and develop a more positive

concern with the adaptation of rural cultural forms to a massive transformation of social experience. An example of a distinctive ethnic culture
which contains such a record of adaptation to new social contexts is the
persistence of Black African musical styles in the musical structure
of Afro-Americans. 'Seen from this broad perspective, the song styles
of Afro-America are, first and foremost, extensions of the cohesive
tradition of African gardeners in the Western hemisphere' (Lomax 1970
p.197). Not only did this distinctive musical culture survive a brutal
transition to slavery and persistent assaults on the cultural integrity of the
slave labour force, it provided a mode of functional adaptation for migrant
workers from the rural South to the urban-industrialized North of
America: 'By replacing the functions served by sacred music, the blues
eased a transition from a land-based agrarian society to one based on
mobile, wage-labour urbanism' (Szwed 1970 p.224). The strength of this
musical culture might suggest that here is an instance of a cultural form
which is located in a community in such a way that it is an important
constituent of the identity of that community. It is undoubtedly true that
there are significant continuities in the varying forms of Afro-American
music (obviously in part because racist discrimination reinforces the ghetto
as cultural enclave), but these continuities do not constitute a folk culture
except as a romantic ideology. The blues, for example, inverted many of
the values of their sacred sources and the blues singer was an ethnic
insider/outsider commenting on the tensions of migration. The blues
therefore provide a bridge over the structural discontinuities of a migrating
labour force, but as these migrants have settled and stabilized, the blues
have been increasingly relegated to a middle-aged, reminiscent audience,
and been supplanted by the more commercially sophisticated soul music
(or adapted to the exigencies of rock music, *cf.* Oliver 1976), so that
Haralambos concludes: 'Despite the evident support for the blues it seems
reasonable to predict that it will die out as a black musical form at least
in northern cities' (1970 p.375). In a paradox familiar to folklorists, if
the blues survive it will be through adoption by young white musicians.

It is relevant in this context to look at the example of British music-
halls in the second half of the nineteenth-century. The example is
appropriate because the halls and their songs were genuinely popular —
both well-attended and seemingly part of a living working-class culture.
The complexity of the example lies in the discontinuity between the
political aspirations of the class and the attitudes and values of popular
performances 'and the difficulty is to explain the emergence of a working-
class culture which showed itself staunchly impervious to middle-class
attempts to guide it, but yet whose prevailing tone was not one of political
combativity, but of an enclosed and defensive conservatism' (Stedman-
Jones 1974 p.462). Stedman-Jones structures his account through a
career profile of three stages which I shall briefly summarize. The first is
the stage of innovation and amateur participation. From 1850 through the

next two decades the number of halls increased very rapidly, although there were large and important halls and 'stars' who travelled between halls, the predominant character of entertainment was small, parochial centres where the neighbours gathered to watch each other perform. 'The vast majority of performers came from poor backgrounds and began by doing turns in pubs or trying themselves out in a newcomer's spot in one of the smaller halls' (*op. cit.* p.490). The second stage is the years between 1870 and 1890 when 'music hall stood for the small pleasures of working-class life . . . and . . . was perhaps the most unequivocal response of the London working class to middle-class evangelism' (*ibid.* pp.490-1). The response is characterized by Stedman-Jones as one of conservative escapism, the entertainment did gently satirize the more prosperous classes and did romanticize the future but these extravagances were firmly rooted in the realities of routine poverty in which 'class is a life-sentence, as final as any caste system' (*op. cit.* p.493). The third stage is a period of decline in terms of vitality although not of profits or attendance. At this stage the halls were generalized out of the slums and became a source of slightly unofficial entertainment for the upper classes, and an opportunity for the dissemination of conservative political attitudes. One indication of the broadening of the audience was a shift in sentiments from populist tones to bombastic jingoism, a shift reinforced by the increasing association betwen Toryism and the drink trade so that the halls came to endorse a style of raffishness rather than class consciousness. The recognition of the commercial respectability of the music halls led to their being incorporated by a syndicate whose policy was to replace the "coarseness and vulgarity" of the halls, by the gentility and decorum of the Palace of Variety' (*op. cit.* p.496). Senelick (1975 p.155) modifies this account by situating the central commercialization as taking place when street broadsides were adapted for more theatrical performance. The conservatism of the art-form is for him more institutionalized and more fundamentally crippling: 'Each of these elements then — the obsolete Licensing Act forbidding seditious polemic, the greater formality and time spent in rehearsing a music-hall act, and the heterogeneity of the audiences, ranging from the restrained well informed to the vociferous illiterate — tended to draw the political teeth of the music-hall song. As a result, very little evidence of innately popular feeling on social issues can be found in them; on the other hand, their instrumentality in forming public opinion may have been immense'.

The commercialization of popular culture is therefore a process in which ethnic and/or communal institutions and forms are 'taken over' and adopted as styles of commodity which can be distributed independently of their original context (thus Balinese village rituals now tour the theatres of the world as performances). For this to be possible the form has to be recognizable as a marketable commodity, and the performers to become 'professionalized' as stars. This process of restyling need not drastically affect the surface appearance of the performance, the history of games and sports provides many examples of the gradual shift from recreation to spectacle (a sympathetic discussion of some aspects of this process as it relates to association football runs through Hopcraft 1971). But even in these cases the narrative stance of the occasion will have been subtly inverted, the public will now participate as an audience.

Although I have separated commercialization and bourgeoisification they are closely related through a common concern with defining appropriate material for different audiences. If we can elucidate the criteria of respectability it may help us to bring out an important strand in the practice of commercialization. The initial example of formulating criteria of respectability I shall discuss is the entrepreneurial initiative shown in quickly adapting the opportunities provided by the development of periodical literature to a female audience (White 1970 chap. 1). The magazine, as a heterogeneous collection of different types of material, was adapted as a journal formula for women so that a 'core of sensation was supplemented with verse, riddles and puzzles, a diary of events at home and abroad, play reviews, and short discourses on topics of general interest, particularly the vulnerability of the female sex to the depravity of the age' (*op. cit.* p.29). This type of literature obviously cannot be described as having anything to do with folk experience and is an indication of the emergence of a commercial popular culture. It is relevant because the history of journalism for a female audience provides a clear instance of the shaping of a developing cultural form by norms of respectability in ways that contributed to the trivialization of the audience — in this case feminine experience. Although eighteenth-century periodicals were frequently sensationalist and trivial it does seem that their readers were assumed to be lively, intelligent people who were interested in all aspects of the social order. In the first decades of the nineteenth century these assumptions were reversed to be replaced by a concentration upon domesticity: 'Women's magazines were no longer required to contribute to the intellectual improvement and advancement of women, merely to provide innocent and amusing reading matter as an alternative to the daily newspapers which were now considered to be too tainted for female perusal' (*op. cit.* p.39). The implication of this change is that the development of suburbanism amongst the middle class was not just a physical segregation but was complemented by a cultural segregation. The latter process took two forms, the first was an increasing emphasis upon forms of respectability as a way of marking polite from brutal society; and secondly a bifurcation of the gender of women into exaggeratedly helpless, pure idols on the one hand and exploited sexual resources on the other (a bifurcation which, as feminist literature has pointed out, has persisted in distorting sexual relationships, particularly in the area of popular culture, to the present day).

It is an appropriate metaphor for the new emphasis on propriety that female dress became increasingly elaborate at this period: periodical literature became dominated by fashion both in response to a demarcated area of female autonomy and because upwardly mobile *nouveaux riches* needed to be socialized into accepted rules of dress and decorum. An emphasis upon restraint and desexualization as criteria of social status helps to illuminate the moral panic over controlling sexual self-exploration in the nineteenth century (*cf.* Comfort 1967), when cruel punishments were inflicted upon children. In such a climate it is more explicable that the response of the pre-Raphaelites and their successors to the cashbox aesthetics of industrialism should have been complemented by pressures to develop art, hygiene and rationality in female dress (*cf.* Newton 1974). Those women who realized the repressive implications of equating femininity with the proprieties of elaborate dress, either sought a solution through greater rationality or through withdrawal into abstracted aesthetics. In correlating the threads that linked respectable segregation from productive labour with the moral encumbrances of elaborate dress, reformers were not of course contributing to popular culture directly. Indeed they probably could not because the rationales for the stress on etiquette, elaborate rules of convention and fashion lay deep in the responses to the social mobility of the nineteenth century, as indices of status formation and change (see Davidoff 1973 for a very interesting discussion of the meaning of polite in this context), and therefore a frontal assault on respectability would have required a commitment to an alternative perception of class relationships. The discontent with respectability as a set of social constraints on women did however help to lay the basis for one of the most persistent stereotypes of popular art — that an index of bohemianism is provided by sartorial carelessness.

It therefore seems to me that the process called bourgeoisification can be understood on at least two levels in this context. The first is an increasing concern with a social hierarchy of respectability which ran throughout the nineteenth century. One rationale for this process is the way in which it provides overt indices of social status; in an era of marked social mobility forms of cultural display provide non-verbal articulation of social position and aspiration. One would therefore expect that once technology made holidays quite widely available there would soon develop a hierarchy of respectable holiday resorts and centres, so that styles of entertainment could be attuned to the status of expected patrons (see for example Walton 1975). The second level is more directly related to the process of suppression to be discussed. It is centrally concerned with recurrent attempts to reform morally the 'brutish' masses so recently gathered in enormous urban slums in the new industrial cities. Given that the 'corollary of free labour was free leisure' the problem of reform was concerned with so organizing leisure-interests that they did not interfere with profitable engagement of labour: 'Contained within the various movements formed to structure working-class leisure one finds approaches to a number of very important and interrelated middle-class objectives:

the preservation of civil order, the imposition of new types of labour-discipline and the diffusion among the working classes of a new (and alien) system of moral authority' (Storch 1977 p.139). Both Storch and Stedman-Jones emphasize that generalizations must be qualified because conditions varied so greatly between cities. But one can say that bourgeois understanding of popular culture has been seen to necessitate a recurrent responsibility to intervene: in the nineteenth century through crusades to reform (Harrison 1967); in the latter half of the twentieth century through crusades to contain (Zurcher and Kirkpatrick 1976; Wallis 1976).

In the paper by Stedman-Jones that has already been cited his discussion of working-class culture provides a suitable introduction to the third mode of incorporation — alienation, as the transformation of the experience of work. This is that the breakdown of the traditional work-centred cultured of London artisans was interrelated with the growth of 'a culture oriented towards the family and the home'. Workers had traditionally lived in the vicinity of their place of work and had participated in a socio-political environment which focussed on the centrality of work customs and adjacent hostelries. This culture was not exclusively masculine but other members of the family were included to the extent that they cooperated with the work community. This background inevitably meant that politics was seen through an occupational focus. In the course of the century a number of factors combined to render political experience both more individual and impersonal. In London the growth of residential suburbs allied with 'The combination of declining industries, the breakdown of skilled crafts into a mass of semi-skilled processes, the prevalence of home work, the decline of a work-centered culture, the growth of commuting and the deadening effects of elementary education made a politically demobilizing impact' (Stedman-Jones 1974 p.489). The process of alienation, as it is understood in this context, is therefore concerned with the interrelationships of the changing experience of work with the institutionalization of a particular style of political activity.

The first sense in which I wish to understand the culture of work is the changing meaning of community. The discussion in the previous paragraph will have introduced the relationship between occupational community and political culture, and it is therefore unsurprising that many of the initial conflicts during the period of rapid industrialization seemed to involve trying to slow the rate of progress. We accept an ideological reading of history at face value, however, if we think of such conflicts as purely sentimental obscurantism, irrationality, and ignore the ways in which, as we saw with the discussion of moral economy, they articulate 'an ethic that presupposes revised notions of art, of community, of culture in the very widest sense' (Meakin 1976 p.17). Once again it is Thompson who alerts us to a metaphoric and physical measure of the restructuring of community: he choose changes in the organization of time in industrial capitalism to embody a process of incorporation: 'What we are examining here are not only changes in manufacturing technique which demand greater synchronization of labour and a greater exactitude in time-routines in *any* society: but also changes as they were lived through in the society of nascent industrial capitalism. We are concerned simultaneously with time-sense in its technological conditioning, and with time-measurement as a means of labour exploitation' (Thompson 1967 p.80). Before large scale machine-powered industry, labour patterns were characteristically irregular, both because the worker retained a degree of autonomy over the rhythm of effort during the day and because the days were more likely to be patterned by bursts of intensive labour followed by idleness. Both of these rhythms were structured by a seasonal calendar, even for those who no longer worked on the land, so that the year was divided by a rich mosaic of festivals and holidays. It would be romantic myopia to deny the existence of exploitation in pre-industrial employment, but the significance of the distinction between labour and play was very different from that between employment and leisure in contemporary experience. When work is cumulated and structured by the participants then time is not just being used and spent but may even be celebrated as an enactment of community.

The direction of this analysis is consistent with an important rethinking of art as human fabrication, but before we draw out this implication I wish to note a second sense of the changing culture of work in industrialization — this is the distinction between machine and tool: 'The machine appears as simply an extension of the tool . . . but in proportion to its increasing efficiency it becomes a means of avoiding contact with nature. Whereas the pre-industrial tool was a way of *making* contact with nature' (Meakin *op. cit.* p.9). From this perspective the division of labour is more than an economic principle for the maximization of efficiency, it involves a transformation of the relationship between man and the product of his consciousness (see the discussion in Clayre's (1974) book which is uneven in quality but does contain some interesting interview material). A recurrent theme in my essay is the concept of fictional distance, the relationship between the author and the narrative he structures; the concept of distance can be a fruitful analogy for the changing use of tools we are trying to pin down here. Instead of tools being extensions of the self which structure and thereby humanize the world to be made, machines provide details to be endlessly repeated so that humanity becomes constituted by mechanical reproduction instead of vice-versa. It is not of course coincidental that fictional distance provides an illuminating analogy because the Marxist critique of the changing meaning of work begins in an aesthetic appreciation of self-realization (Lifshitz 1973). In his discussion of literature and industrialization Meakin correctly points to the relationship between Ruskin and Morris as being of crucial importance in clarifying in the course of the nineteenth century how culture could be art-ful labour, and in this way the past can be used as a progressive model for the future. Medievalism provided a critical lever in the mid-nineteenth century to 'open-up' the ways in which the making of art could be an analytic frame for the making of society. 'The medieval workman, argues Ruskin, lending his eloquence to the creation of a potent myth — was free *in his work,* however rigid the social hierarchy in which he laboured; and this freedom in work made him into an artist' (Meakin *op. cit.* p.44). The alienation of cultural experience complements the other modes of incorporation already discussed in that the cumulative impact of these processes is to transform a performance into a commodity which articulates a narrow, highly predictable and stylized, segment of experience.

The modes of incorporation discussed so far have been concerned with changing cultural forms. The last heading to be discussed, suppression, is more concrete than the others and is less concerned with change in style than disappearance of substance. The key is once again provided by Thompson: 'The preliminaries to the industrial revolution were so long that, in the manufacturing districts in the early eighteenth century, a vigorous and licensed popular culture had evolved, which the propagandists of discipline regarded with dismay' (1967 p.80). The three key words in that sentence in relation to this discussion are vigorous, licensed and dismay. Malcolmson (1973) in his book on popular recreations in the eighteenth and early nineteenth centuries, does much to elucidate in particular vigorous and licensed. The points made will be familiar to some extent from the preceeding discussion: not only was the work culture less specific to occupations and embraced a wider swathe of social experience, the pattern of work within the culture was characteristically intermittently intensive, and periods of rest were celebrations which occasionally exploded in seasonal festivals — exploded because such festivals were feared as bacchanalian routs. The conflicting perspectives on eighteenth-century popular culture were therefore a traditionalist view on the one hand which licensed a vigorous barbarism in which the local gentry often joined with social inferiors, opposed by progressives who found the mixture of licentiousness shocking, who were dismayed by the collective riotousness of such public gatherings, and who were appalled by wasting time in irrational holidays particularly when celebrated in inebriation.

An interesting paper dealing with the mechanisms of interventionism comes in Storch's discussion of the role of policemen in northern English towns: 'Many nineteenth-century contemporaries specifically linked the coming of the police to the decline of traditional customs and amusements . . . . It would be absurd to advance any single explanation for nineteenth-century transformations of popular culture, but there is no question that interventions of the police and of those who directed them played a considerable role' (1976 pp.492, 493). The basis of these claims concerning the significance of police as domestic missionaries derives from the police acting as the vanguard of a widespread attempt to impose urban discipline. The new magistracies and local elites of the rapidly expanding industrial towns were generally representatives of the rationalism of political economy, their targets were those aspects of the activities and recreations of their labour force which either interfered with profitable employment or facilitated organization to resist the conditions of employment. The ostensible desire to improve the habits of the lower classes was given impetus and fervour by the realization that the new urban masses had a distinct culture, which was so inexplicable as to threaten to destroy the structural foundations of the emergent social order. This is not the place to rehearse details of specific types of intervention, their success is shown by the almost total disappearance of traditional customs and festivals from English industrial life — not so much because such practices became somehow evolutionarily inappropriate, as is the explanatory theme of contemporary commentators, but because participants were harassed and prosecuted; even occasionally thwarted by the presence of the military.

The willingness to use quite a considerable display of force in dealing with such customs indicates that the significance of popular culture in this respect is related to the issue of control. The political community was manifestly changing its bases, membership and structure, the nature of the control which was to be exercised by the new elites had to be debated and the contradictions in the ideology of economic freedom had to be resolved. It is for these reasons that the struggle in the first decades of the nineteenth century for the government to allow an unstamped press, and the rhetoric of the illegal press which circulated amongst a largely proletarian audience are particularly interesting (for a wide-ranging although unsophisticated version of the struggles to 'free' the press see Harrison 1974). The struggle arose because the ideology of freedom of expression could be seen to be in conflict with accounts of society based on working-class interests. The 'solution' to this conflict was to encourage 'responsible' (respectable) political debate divorced from too close commitments to class as opposed to party perspectives.

During the first thirty years of the century the predominant government response was to use the controlling powers of first the Home Office and then the Treasury to regulate the modes of public discourse. A series of setbacks allied with both Parliamentary and national pressures disillusioned successive governments and led to new sources of stability. Hollis (1970, conclusion) lists five ways in which the debate over the regulation of newspapers was significant: it was part of a wider debate over public education as a mode of incorporation; the struggle for a cheap press 'opened up a new field in cheap literature for the masses'; the campaign for an unstamped press had a number of important middle-class supporters; but, fourthly, the working class campaigned in its own right; while finally, some aspects of the press developed new political and economic theory. The campaign for an unstamped press is therefore important because it illustrates how an initial attempt at suppression was modified by commercializing one form of public discourse and thereby extending the consensus over the boundaries of political form: 'To extend to those already engaged in politics was to stabilize the system. The larger the political community, the greater the area that was subject to the divide and rule of politics . . . To become a "recognized portion of public opinion" was to become paid-up members of the political community' (Hollis *op. cit.* p.306).

In order fully to understand suppression as a mode of incorporation in relation to popular culture we have to divide the process into three types. The first is explicit outlawing; the second is ghettoization — tolerance if the activity is confined to a closed community; and modified acceptance, as when a popular press is allowed when there is agreement over the limits to expression. The type I have called ghettoization is interesting because it poses distinctive problems for dominant elites. For example, the role of fundamentalist faiths amongst the Black communities in North America has been largely functional for the social order. It has been a distinctive popular cultural form and yet it has encouraged concern with other-worldly salvation and had not promoted dissent. And yet since 1945 the forms of popular faith have been adapted to secular politics both in terms of a very strong religious leadership in civil rights struggles, and in terms of a rhetorical style borrowed from religious occasions. The salience of the 'private' religious culture to political mobilization has undoubtedly encouraged a racial consciousness which has been dys-functional for the dominant political order. There is therefore a recurrent uneasiness amongst administrative elites concerning distinctive or private cultural forms amongst subordinate groups; although the process is to some extent inevitable because, as Storch amongst others points out, the characteristic response of subordinates to control is evasion and there is therefore a tremendous resilience in popular institutions. As a concluding example I wish merely to note the status of linguistic diversity in con-temporary industrial societies. Regional dialects and registers are examples of limited cultural forms which one would imagine to be politically innocuous and even occasions for sentimental retrieval (folk relics in urban environments). They are, however, potential bases for alternative communal identity and as such indices of regional or class autonomy. At this stage I do not wish to engage in the debate about the educational implications of class variations in speech styles, but many of the points we have made about incorporating popular culture obviously are at least analogous to the perception of lower-class speech as a social problem.

Public Space

In the course of this chapter I have made some preliminary notes on the interaction between forms of communication (cultural expression) and opportunities for political participation. I have used the idea of publics as political collectivities to illuminate the nature of audiences for entertainment. The force of an analogy between public and audience is that we come to understand the expressions of will of the former as an earlier form of the careless choices of the latter; or more forcefully that the myopia induced by the trivialization of entertainment precludes thoughtful political participation. The sociological response has too frequently consisted of a technical attempt to develop a research methodology to measure degrees of deception and delusion. This approach is inappropriate because it transforms the social opportunities of audience membership into an empirical problem of the potential power of messages to shape consciousness. A more positive approach is to explore the opportunities of membership — the ways in which public experience is practically put together as involvement with cultural performances. As we have seen, there are significant features of the contemporary manufacture of public communication which operate to impoverish consciousness, and thereby collective experience, but despairingly to accept the inevitability of impoverishment is to ignore the implications of manufacture. To cooperate in cultural transactions is to engage with the terms of fictional possibility and thereby constitute identity. Thus we must ask how is it possible to accomplish the emergence of alternative public styles?

I propose to take up another aspect of public life as it relates to communication in urban-industrial society. The definition which was used to begin this book on popular art involved stressing the urban character of popular experience, and a recapitulation of this definitional theme has involved an extended exploration of significant changes in the transformation from folk to popular experience. I have therefore already made an important commitment to the centrality of urbanism in any study of popular art. I believe it to be appropriate at this stage to make this commitment explicit and look at some of the ways in which urbanism as the organization of social space could be relevant to the significance of cultural forms. (I should say at the beginning that as with the discussion of the literature on mass communication, the literature on urban sociology will be rifled very selectively and very largely ignored; this is not arrogance but because I am only concerned with urban forms as ways of life.) Our physical environment is a resource that is usually considered as economic, occasionally as aesthetic but only rarely as cognitive. It is of course true that the recent development of a concern with the environment as a political issue has involved some fundamental reconsideration of unequal access and exploitation of that which should be held in common. When it is realized that the politics of the environment involves equivalent concerns with other political practices then the economic organization of physical resources comes to be understood as part of the wider organization of productive resources in society. Politicizing the environment does involve thinking through the social implications of access and exploitation, but the organization of space is not explored as an exemplification of cultural distinctions — as for example when landscape architecture is recognized as aesthetic shaping of an environment so that it can become a display of cultural values of order opposed to savagery (Lubove 1975).

The most available instance of the social organization of symbolic space derives from the practice of architecture; although it is true that most architectural theory approaches the study of effective design through aesthetic concepts rather than a concern with cultural values. An example of a study that does adopt the latter approach comes in Bourdieu's analysis of the living arrangements in a Berber household (1973). In this study he uses structuralist analysis to show the interrelationships between rules of use and the hierarchical arrangement of household members. It becomes possible to see the divisions we make between rooms with different functions, between the inside and outside, between public and private and particularly the ways we organize specialist areas relating to bodily functions as symbolic statements articulating important aspects of different forms of sharing (Mary Douglas has engaged this topic very provocatively on a number of occasions, perhaps most relevantly in Douglas 1970 although see also some of the essays in Douglas 1975). From this perspective our physical environment is saturated with meaning and we have no reason to believe that the social symbolism of space is confined to the environments controlled by household units. The space between households, literally the grounds upon which our communities are drawn, is equally a symbolic terrain, an area on which the rules of communal form can be dramatically displayed. It is perhaps a good example of the characteristic blindness of ideological thought, that the dominance of aesthetic and engineering concerns in the development of the architectural profession's understanding of its proper responsibilities led to it being a 'startling discovery' that the organization of public space in contemporary urban design was an inducement to vandalism (Newman 1972). It would seem to me that this could only be hidden from professional theorists when those theorists were blinkered by a series of ideological conceptions of public life and expectations for public space.

My argument is that if we are to develop any sense of the interrelationships of popular art as lived aesthetics with the constitution of public life as communal experience, we must pay some attention to the cultural geography of urban society. The classic statements in this field were formulated through a concern with urban geography and its implications for the individual psyche. The thesis of classical urban sociology, I am thinking here of the tradition which runs from German theorists such as Tonnies and Simmel through the work of the Chicago school, was that structural changes in social geography produce cultural changes in modes of interaction and even cognition, thus: 'The Metropolis and Mental Life'. I note this point because too often the significance of urbanism is understood to be the implications of scale and heterogeneity for the number of relationships an individual might conventionally engage in. This emphasis is undoubtedly present, the contrast against which metropolitan experience is drawn is an idealized village conception of folk society, but it is not the only or even the main theme in characterizing urban life: 'The most significant aspect of the metropolis lies in this functional magnitude beyond its actual physical boundaries' (Simmel 1971 p.335). Metropolitan life, from this perspective, involves restructuring the cultural categories through which we order and begin to interpret routine experience.

Critical reactions to what I have described as the classical thesis of urbanism can be grouped under three headings. The first is the most straight-forward and covers criticisms that are concerned with the empirical validity of an account of urbanism based on specific features of central urban districts. Thus it is argued that Wirth based his account on ghetto areas which are inappropriate models for suburban life, that such is the rate of change in urban living patterns that any generalization will be quickly obsolete, and that where the classic characterization still seems relevant it relates to groups disturbed by residential instability. Under the second, an inappropriate connection is seen to be made between structural relationships and individual understanding, a way of life is being conceived in inappropriately psychologistic terms. To some extent this criticism derives from changes in fashions in conceptual vocabulary, 'mental life' now has unfortunate connotations, but it does point to a persistent problem for the symbolic interactionist tradition — the extent to which studies of interaction necessarily draw on interpretive stereo- types which are left unexamined. Under the third heading, the thesis depends upon the use of normative categories as if they were empirical categorizations. The main example is the idealization of folk society as a *gemeinschaft* predecessor for contemporary *anomie*. Not only do such conceptions involve mystifying our understanding of both the past and the processes of historical transformation through which structural change is accomplished, but they also provide a basis for an ideological conception of desirable social forms in contemporary society.

I have briefly described these three types of criticism to make clear that in order to continue with a discussion of urbanism and public life, we must be sensitive to the ideological implications of different modes of conceptualizing characteristic relationships. The importance of the classical thesis is that it tries to illuminate the interconnections between cultural geography, shared manners within a collectivity, and the terms held in common for participating in public ceremonies, the institutionalization of a distinctive public culture. This public culture is so rooted in urban industrialism that its structural features and problems can come to seem distinctive, even defining features of public culture. I am thinking for example of the problem of social order which has been seen to be the central problematic of sociological analysis; the concept of social order is most mystically conceived when it is described as public order — the adherence to implicit norms of conduct in public space. Thus the connection that is made in practice between political demonstrations and commercial vice such as prostitution and pornographic bookshops. When

public life is understood normatively it is always an ideal to be defended
against infractions possible in the anonymity of an urban environment.
Other features of public culture which can be seen as deriving from the
implications of urban industrialization are the stress on rationality as
instrumentally oriented grounds for debate and cooperation, so that
bourgeois politics as one sense of public life may be defended as rational
empiricism; and, finally, a concern with civility as a set of norms regulating
interaction — so that a characteristic restraint may be seen as public form
in contrast with private intimacy.

The sociologist who has most distinctively engaged themes in the
formal organization of public culture has been Erving Goffman. The
conventional characterization of his work by his colleagues has been in
terms of dramatism as theory and metaphor. I do not believe an equation
of public and drama to be completely mistaken but it exploits a reified
conception of drama and always seems to invite the criticism that the
analytic stance in which the equation is made is insincere, even cynical. I
do not want to discuss Goffman's work in terms of its use of dramatic
analogies, nor his cynicism — although I will argue that there is a significant normative dimension to his perspective — but rather his analysis of
being in public to elucidate the negotiation of cultural geography (no
attempt will be made to survey the entire corpus of Goffman's publications — I utilize only some aspects of the papers in Goffman 1971). The
paper on normal appearances begins with the significant distinction
between the world as it is when taken for granted and significant features
of that world when it is scanned for cues for alarm: 'The individual's
Umwelt can be defined as the region around him from within which signs
for alarm can come' (*op. cit.* p.297). The scanner's responses to such cues
are derived from what he can habitually handle, the threat inherent in the
breakdown of normality is that an individual will lose control and he may
doubt his competence to recover. In practice the nightmare of a menacing,
incomprehensible environment is a terror that is more usually exploited as
a fictional resource rather than an everyday experience; we buy out of
privacy by making an investment in manipulating appearance so that we
create, as Goffman says, a 'normalcy show, a show in which all participants
have the task of acting unfurtively'. The most fundamental concern of
everyday interaction is therefore with creating and sustaining the surface
character of public order, social space is exploited and negotiated through
routines of civility so that aggression and other Hobbesian impulses are
channeled through sanctioned forms.

The constitutive interaction of self and presentation with which
Goffman is concerned goes beyond interaction to how identity is constituted. One can see this more clearly if the play on 'place' in Goffman's
essays is brought out: we realize that place is not just physical position or
social status but the web of shared assumptions which order civility:
'Through socialization into group living, the individual comes in effect to

make assumptions about himself. . . . These assumptions about himself concern his normatively supported place in the group' (*op. cit.* p.398). When the individual sees himself as others do he will strive to structure his appearances as ones they will recognize as normal, or routine, so that he can take himself for granted: 'His show of being safely disattendable is deeply him; he has no self that is deeper, although he has some that are as deep' (*op. cit.* p.328). Goffman is able to clothe this conception of self as civility with a characteristically savage joke in which the elan of the comparison assuages to some extent the bitterness which prompted it: 'A person with carcinoma of the bladder can, if he wants, die with more social grace and propriety, more apparent inner social normalcy, than a man with a harelip can order a piece of apple pie' (*op. cit.* p.409). If the argument that the self is constituted through acceptance by others is granted then it becomes possible for Goffman is to extend the significance of place by making the claim that 'mental symptoms' are not inappropriate ideas but 'situational improprieties': 'The concern of the family is not simply that a member has crazy notions, but that he is not keeping his place in relationships' (*op. cit.* p.422). I therefore argue that Goffman's concern with the appearance of normality is not another descriptive approach to the negotiation of interaction, but might be better described as an analysis of the deep structure of social grammar: it is through our ability to conform to the restraints of situational proprieties that we are able to avoid the horror, 'the deep embarrassment', of being out of place: 'The most disruptive thing a person can do is fail to keep a place that others feel can't be changed for him' (*op. cit.* p.449).

The metaphor of place for the constitutive development of self is a linguistic resource which trades on a series of assumptions only possible in urban industrial society. The metaphor is not misplaced or inappropriate, but it makes sense in relation to an understanding of public culture which has not been explicated. The basis of this relationship is through the common reliance of place and public upon rules of sensible form: the lack of structural restrictions on access to public life (the consumer democracy of symbolic politics) means that civility becomes 'the implicit moral requirement for viable social life'. The obverse of the constitutive significance of civility for place and public is that the situational impropriety of personal insanity can become on the level of the society at large a decline of civility such that there is 'an attenuation of that degree of restraint which preserves individual integrity and social order'. (This and the previous quotation come from Manning 1976, which provides an interesting introduction to Goffman's terrors of minimal respect.) When the restraints of public order cease to be sufficient for adequate security, the typical member of society Goffman postulates as his subject, has to be constantly sensitive to his own vulnerability. When in the presence of others (and of course we always are) the subject must be constantly aware that: 'They can intend to rob him, assault him, sexually molest him, or

block his free movement' (Goffman *op. cit.* p.354); and as 'an apparently
undesigned contact can turn out in retrospect to have been the first visible
move in a well-designed game being planned against the individual, . . . it
follows that *any* current incidental contact that has not so far led to anything alarming might indeed do so' (*op. cit.* p.375). The jungle analogies
Goffman is fond of have a resonance beyond the ecological bases of social
life — the public culture of urban experience is melodramatic such that
the genre becomes a root metaphor for the whole analytic exercise.
Existential insecurity is not limited to subjects but is inherent in all urban
experience so that 'the others' (Goffman seems to share a Kafkaesque
inability to name the threatening presence): ' . . . others . . . in the role of
predator . . . have to be concerned about normal appearances. . . . They are
forced to become phenomenologists, close students of everyday life, not,
of course, their own but what the subject takes to be everyday experience'
(*op. cit.* p.306).

It would be inappropriate to attempt to decide whether urban
experience is in fact more dangerous for those engaged in routine use now
than it was one hundred or two hundred years ago. This is because
Goffman's approach is abstracted from history — the constitutive interaction of self and place is presented as a topic in its own right. Such an
abstraction is not a cynical concern with theatricality, more a deep moral
horror at the destructive implications of social embarrassment so that
limits of social ambition become the preservation of stability and reliability. The central criticism of such an analytic stance is not that it mistakes
the character of relations in public life, but that the analysis is conducted
in terms of a passive understanding: 'the inability to imagine social relations
which would arouse much passion, an imagination of public life in which
people behave, and manage their behaviour, only through withdrawal,
"accommodation", and "appeasement" ' (Sennett 1976 p.36). So far in
this discussion I have taken it for granted that public refers to 'space'
shared in common, that its natural contrast is to the private sphere — that
shared with the members of one's family or other close social intimates.
This distinction is not the only possible one, however; in terms of West
European usage between the Renaissance and the Enlightenment 'public'
changes from a reference to the common good to a region of social life.
The impetus for change can be located in the interaction of changing
political forces with the development of cosmopolitan urban centres which
afforded opportunities for the exercise of taste and sophistication. If we
accept that the conception of public life as a distinct mode of sociability
is contingent upon specifiable historical conditions, then it follows that
further changes in those conditions will have implications for the
character of public sociability. And, despite qualifications, the Goffmanite
characterization of contemporary public life as an infinitely precarious
appeasement is persuasive (particularly if we bear in mind the architectural
conception of public space as areas for communication as transmission

rather than for communication as participation), then it follows that we should attend to changes in the staging of public culture.

The impetus for change is likely to be a consequence of changing political relationships through new facilities for entertainment and leisure. The politics of display in which gross audiences are invited to applaud or condemn competing casts of actors as leaders is a mode of public life in which the problems of scale are resolved by dissolving the centre (stage or arena). The interaction between the provision of entertainment through the use of centralized facilities of mass communication and the development of a politics of display turns on the staging of collective ceremonies as performances for individuals so that 'the mass media infinitely heighten the knowledge people have of what transpires in the society, and they infinitely inhibit the capacity of people to convert that knowledge into political action' (Sennett *op. cit.* p.283). There is a recurrent paradox that as metropolitan provision swamps regional variation, so that we seem to live more in a world of shared forms, there is an increasing emphasis upon retreating from public civility to private individual experience. The reasons for the paradox are: the licence for deviance possible when the public arena is conceptualized as a mingling-ground for strangers means that the arena becomes associated with its reputation so that use of public facilities can come in itself to seem suspicious (thus the famous suspicion of Los Angeles policemen with regard to pedestrians); secondly, a political climate of futility and cynicism when public affairs seem beyond the reach of the audience and the privileged are seen cynically to tailor their performances; and finally, there is the response to the complexities of contemporary social order which substitutes psychological criteria of authenticity in place of the forms of social civility: 'The more this localizing rules, the more people seek out or put pressure on each other to strip away the barriers of custom, manners, and gesture which stand in the way of frankness and mutual openness' (*op. cit.* p.338).

The paradox of public space in this the most public of societies is therefore that the facilities for collective experience are viewed with suspicion, even terror. Enormous energy and capital resources are poured into developing the mass production of technology for private access to public communication — for example television that most domestic of media. Sennett describes the translation of public culture into private experience as the ideology of intimacy, in which the complexities of social reality are interpreted by contemporaries through psychological categories of authenticity, frankness and mutual openness. One aspect of this process is the ideology of communication discussed in the first section, that social problems are inherently due to failures of communication. Such a naive faith in the efficacy of articulation is maintained in a culture marked by huge industries of communication which effectively operate to render everybody an audience, listeners, to themselves. (The resolution of this paradox is only possible through a realization that communication is not speaking, etc., as a process in itself, but about a self-conscious structure of speech, a civility of discourse. We may then accept Steiner's observation that the essence of language is the facility it provides for misinformation, fiction, juggling with the form of reality.) Sennett suggests that another paradox of authenticity inherent in the ideology of intimacy concerns the character of contemporary eroticism. Reacting against the taboos of Victorian repression we have come to view sexuality as a root metaphor for identity so that restraints of convention would be an alienation of self, not realizing, however, that in making this equation we enter into an infinite regress of an endless search for revelation: 'We do not today learn 'from' sex, because that puts sexuality outside of the self; instead, we unendingly and frustratingly go in search of ourselves through the genitals' (*op. cit.* p.7).

A feature of an ideology of intimacy, where public culture is conceptualized as a forum for private experience, will be performances which articulate audience narcissism, as a state of being continually sought in which form reflects intimate needs (as well as Sennett's discussion of narcissism as actors deprived of their art; see also Lasch (1976) on a contemporary cultural malaise). In relation to my theme of the public geography of cultural space, intimacy and narcissism will interact through a concern with communalism – the community as the social form for private experience in which the menace and insincerity of public relations are filtered by the autonomy of status shared in common. It is possibly unfair to put on the same continuum the status enclaves of commuter villages as quasi-communities to which the inhabitants retreat and the self-conscious communes fostered by the search for an alternative society. And yet the shared cultural form is there – throughout the continuum the locus for meaningful experience is sought within a private version of social life rather than public forms for personal experience. The inversion is important because for those who would situate themselves at one end of the continuum the experiments in communalism are seen to have political implications, the personal forms are presaging an alternative public order. It is from this stand point that we can begin to reflect on the legacy of the cultural politics of the sixties. The revival of fashionable interest in popular art in recent years has not been purely a magazine marketing of imagery as commodities (in which period junk can be continually cannibalized as material for fashionable display), but has also been due to the conviction that recapturing popular art by the people would be a gigantic political assault on the norms of cultural order which sustain conventional society. If this conviction has any substance then obviously popular art is not just a medium of class incorporation but may also be a means of emancipation.

One reason for suggesting that the cultural revolution of generational politics is best understood from the perspective of the cultural geography of public life is that the revolution presumed economic emancipation. It is too glib to say that it was (is?) purely the politicization of middle-class life style, (important sources of imagery and cultural models were drawn from ghetto experience), but the transformation of life style rather than vice-versa. The initial impetus of the critique was therefore to liberate consciousness, to authenticate stardom by rendering public image as synonymous with private personality. Such a rewriting of cultural aspirations had two main strands, the first was bohemian impatience with the 'stifling' conventions of polite society and in the traditional bohemian manner much of the imagery for this rejection was sought amongst the despised inhabitants of urban centres — so that the ambiguities of public space were both a gathering ground and a metaphor for the alternative society; the second was the conviction that the final defensible bastion against bourgeois (straight) hegemony was the privacy of individuality — personal expression and understanding. It was less clearly appreciated that the pursuit of such aspirations involved supplanting social form with cultural form — a romanticism in which the audience for the emerging arts was also the cast. Elsewhere (chapter 3, section 4) I discuss the nature of stardom in contemporary entertainment, but the idea of the star as involving a distinctive type of heroism is relevant here. I argue that the idea of a star is misunderstood if thought of as an idealization or a role-model, rather stars exist to help define the lived world, help constitute a range of possibilities. The stars of the counter-culture took emancipation from the constraints of conventional responsibilities for granted and thus liberated could explore themselves as opportunities for authenticity. In such a strictly experimental way the heroes of the alternative society could be said to transcend the forms of conventional politics, their qualification being the achievement of a set of scenes (in both senses) for which there is no clear narrative structure.

To say this, however, may be saying nothing more than the 'traditional left' critique of bohemianism — that its laudable impulse lacks the discipline of historical analysis. In the cultural politics of the 1960s this starting-point was overlaid by extending the concepts 'bourgeois' and 'domination' to become general metaphors for convention and stability, allied with the conviction that emancipation was at least as much individual as collective. In this context radicalism was understood to be doing more than writing a new chapter in history books, more as substituting a new text in which the life forms of the future society were first articulated as performances which paradoxically rehearsed everyday experience. To clarify the point, it seems to me that the symbolic dramas of the alternative society — such as festivals — were enactments of the revolution accomplished, and yet such dramas drew on and staged (enacted) a widely-practiced life style. An example of the inter-active process I am thinking of is provided by the significance of the body in counter-cultural thought. To some extent changes in consciousness of the body are part of a recasting of sexuality which has been variously described as 'the new permissiveness' or 'the sexual revolution', in which one literally displays authenticity by a refusal to be bound by taboos on body visibility or functions. In such cases one can say that the body has become a medium for important elements in the ideology of intimacy discussed above. More significantly the body may be used as a metaphor for social and cultural relationships. For example, the body may be seen as referent for sexual identity (cf. Hyman 1976), or as a model for the community so that new means of communication are sometimes held to extend the body as an image for new modes of communal interaction. (Papers which have considered the body as medium and metaphor for the counter-culture are O'Neill 1972 and Benthall 1976; see also Youngblood 1970 and for a more 'straight' discussion of the significance of changes in body presentation Firth 1973.) Through such imagery a political style developed in which new modes of relationship could be understood as enacting an alternative social order — a liberation of imagination which entailed a transformation of society.

There are three types of connection between cultural politics and the more general theme of public space. The first is the ways in which the rejection of conventional society is an extension of the privatization of public politics. When public life comes to be seen as insincere, ambiguous or possibly dangerous one response is to withdraw into a world of relationships characterized by non-public values, and to use this world as a model for recommended reforms of public life. One can see that aspects of populist traditionalism correspond to this description and it may be for this reason that some commentators have seen the counter-culture as essentially conservative (in retrospect the novels of culture-hero Ken Kesey read as celebrations of frontier values). The second connection lies in the counter-cultural stress upon authenticity, unfettered individuality, as the basis for a way of life; in this respect civility has been translated from codes of conduct to mutual respect. Whether or not one believes that the rewriting of individualism in the underground involved a serious consideration of the problems of egalitarianism, it is true that a politics of style was expressed through a form of collectivity which is more usefully described as tribalization rather than in terms of traditional stratification. This then is the third connection between the politics of counter-culture and public space that the mobility of metropolitan society, both psychic and physical, became a means of emancipation — as in the imagery of 'urban gypsies': the self-description of members as travellers and the importance of pilgrimage as a form of apprenticeship. In such a mobile environment it is unremarkable that forms of association came to be thought of as tribes brought together by shared cultural styles. The members of a tribe, and for only the most enthusiastic must tribes be mutually exclusive, constitute a community of taste in which public space is reshaped in terms of the themes of that association — for example a map of drug access and use will be a very focused structuring of the urban environment. (There is of course by now an enormous bibliography on the counter-culture but some of the more sympathetic texts are Berke 1969; Musgrove 1974; Stansill and Mairowitz 1971; and Roszak 1968.)

In using a concept of tribalization I do not wish to imply just a reference to McLuhan's celebration of the implications of changing technology creating a global village, where aesthetic appreciation constitutes the total environment — a very privatized view of public experience. Tribalism does connote a loose sense of primary communalism, a relatively stable social unit whose members are known to one another and whose experience is structured by traditional forms — forms which seem to many to have an aura of natural authenticity. Another aspect of tribalism I wish to emphasize is that suggested by traditional aesthetic forms: in the same ways in which ethnographers of folk cultures have analysed the structures of oral traditions — so the festivals, rituals and symbolic forms of the counter-culture should be amenable to ethnographic analysis. My reason for saying this is not just that members of the counter-culture consciously ape primitivism, but because it seems that much of the redefinition of experience they are engaged in is concerned with communitas as the initial impulse to sociality rather than structure as the patterning of modes of relationship. Communitas is usually enacted in those circumstances when the boundaries of social structure are reached, most typically the great life-crises such as birth, marriage and death, when communal integration is often articulated by the participants stripping away the marks of status both hierarchical and sexual. It is possible to see much of the imagery of the counter-culture as more or less consciously striving to reenact communitas — by aping the appearance of mendicants, by minimizing sexual difference, by emphasizing cathartic occasions in which revelatory 'knowledge' could be attained, and by obliterating the forms of conventional social order such as the means of marking the passing of time (cf. the papers by Weider and Zimmerman 1974; Shepherd 1972; and Horton 1967).

If we take seriously the aspirations to changing cultural forms also described as generational politics in the years since 1945, then the interaction of imagery, public forms and means of association make it inappropriate to picture the decay of the counter-culture as the inevitable consequence of mistaken politics. It is necessary that aspirations to communalism are unsustainable and become supplanted by institutionalized structural practices; but a consequence of communal fervour is likely to be a continuing dissatisfaction with the presuppositions of such practices (for example the influence of counter-cultural values in consideration of access to media of public communication and thus the significance of the 'underground' press and fights to gain community control of access to cable television and video facilities etc.). Another legacy is the realization that the communalism of the counter-culture was not just a romantic eccentricity, but derived from and is only explicable in relation to the historical interaction of the development of metropolitan centres with the provision of popular art. In this context the most significant feature of the cultural politics of radical bohemias is that they have overlapped with elements in the style and themes of more conventional popular art. An important element in contemporary sensibility is articulated through the opportunity popular art provides to constitute community. The forms of social space through which our collectivities are experienced are, in a variety of ways, made tangible by our means of communication and cultural organization. The pushing at the edges of normality inherent in counter-cultural ambition emphasized the extent that 'realities' of public experience are in an important sense 'fictions' of dramatic staging. It is for this reason that I conclude this chapter at this point and take up in the next some aspects of the significance of realism to popular art in industrial societies.

3

Paradoxes of Realism

Fictional Knowledge

I have argued that the most fruitful perspective on popular culture begins with the social organization of making and distributing art. It is implicit in this approach that the boundaries between different styles of symbolic representation are themselves recommendations for different types of practical attention, and the accomplishment of formulating and sustaining such boundaries in different social contexts is inextricably part of the organization of experience in those contexts. In order to develop this argument I now have to pay more attention to the performances and what they represent as well as their style of representation. It is because our fictional experience is structured by the social organization of access to productive resources that our conceptual vocabularies bespeak relations of power, property and production. Despite the interdependence of the sociology of art with the sociology of knowledge, in everyday experience we do make an important distinction between referential statements in epistemology and symbolic representations. It may be that the ways in which we represent our experience to ourselves is a way of knowing the world, but the 'knowledge' articulated in such representations is not equatable with knowing how, for example, to build a motor car. Another way of putting the same point is to say that if the conceptual vocabulary of conventional knowledge is a set of labels, then the labelling that is going on in symbolic representation differs in certain crucial respects. In order to further our understanding of what we are doing when we engage in making art we need to pay further attention to the claim that there are crucial differences in ways of labelling the world.

I will suggest that there are two main ways in which we can appreciate how art as a way of knowing differs from other forms of knowledge. The first concerns the collective expectations of those who engage in staging performances as opposed to their expectations in more instrumental interaction; the second concerns communicative interaction as modes of humanizing our environment, as ways of rendering it malleable and accessible. I shall discuss each in turn. It is conventional to think of a real world which stretches out from us with endless ramifications, and a fictional world where the ramifications of actions are bounded by the conventions of performance. Thus although the monster on the screen may be as terrifying as he would be in real life we know that we can always get up and leave the cinema, whereas presumably the residents of Transylvania could not leave the country *en masse*. If, however, we try to be slightly more specific about the ways in which fictional action differs from real action the distinction appears less clear cut. The reason for this is that it is misleading to assume that that which is real can be equated with that which is self-evident. The literature on the ways in which reality is a social construct is by now too voluminous to be aptly surveyed here, it is sufficient to note that our confidence in a self-evident world is an artful construction which needs continuous negotiation and reassurance.

Given that this is so, reality is not a non-problematic given — something which straightforwardly provides a context for our imaginings, I would rather say that it is a more or less consistent set of conventional judgements on ways of attending to possible experience. Thus our everyday world is not only *a selection* of significant phenomena it is *an engagement* through time. Reality is a continuous process of the actualization of possibilities, it is a sense of future relevance as much as taken for granted features of an everyday world. The contrast between illusion and reality is not that one is more intensely true than the other, or any other sense of authentic. Illusions are misleading because if acted upon at some point they will fail to correspond to others' expectations and thus rupture the social fabric. (The frailty of these boundaries is exposed when a charismatic leader with sufficient faith in his own 'illusions' is able to render them 'real', for example Lenin.) The final test of the real-ness of a characterization must lie in the relevant social consensus that it is an appropriate characterization: it may seem obvious to us that we can reread the reality of primitive medicine (account for what is really going on), but its efficacy does not depend on our reading. In the light of this discussion we can say that fictional representations differ from reality only in the collective expectations of those who engage in their production. 'There is no objective reality to "copy" or "imitate" but only a selection from that reality in terms of the kinds of practical and symbolic activities in which we engage. . . . For the child, as for the creative artist, the use of the culture involves the process of expanding and refining the code, of defining "lawful" or "comprehensible" or "possible" options as he goes. This is the heart of the skill in the use of symbolic codes' (Bruner and Olsen 1973 p.222).

A fictional performance comprises human actions, whatever the medium of expression and whatever the topic; the act of representation is rendering it human — amenable to human use. Even the most abstract or random display is humanized by its production and more commonly fictions involve a retelling of human actions or aspects of human experience. At the heart of representation, however, it is curiously inanimate; the narrative unfolds as it does at our whim and could be changed. Of course the more we are permanently members of different audiences the more our narratives seem autonomous, impervious to our wishes (thus the force of ceremonials). But we recognize that this autonomy is a function of the production of entertainment in any society, some people are authors, and authorship necessarily involves control over the narrative (perhaps this is why ceremonials like contemporary sport seem to be authorless). If therefore we compare the constitutive interaction in producing a performance it is apparent that it is a mode of human action as real as any other action, but the product of these acts, although it depicts human themes, is deemed inanimate in its human context because the point when the performance becomes a product is continually subject to human control.

The reason I have emphasized that fiction is not less real than any other part of the everyday world is that I want to claim that the knowledge of the world embodied in fictional report (symbolic representation) is not necessarily less true than the knowledge embodied in a technical account. It does not differ in degree of truth but in the uses to which knowledge can be put. A fictional performance is only compelling while its claims to animation are treated seriously; we turn away, dismiss it as a product, and the animation evaporates. While it lives for us we understand our world in a further way, a technical account on the other hand does not depend on our breathing in life. We have to judge it appropriate of course as well as consistent etc., but it has been devised to be used to attain some goal even if it is only intellectual self-aggrandisement. We may prefer knowledge which is elegantly phrased but the rationale is functional, fictions are not centrally valued for their utility. Indeed part of the force of fictional representation is the aura of self-sufficiency spun round the constituent human actions of production so that it is attended to seriously as model for emulation.

It is a feature of the ideology of aestheticism that the aura of self-sufficiency can be reified so that the 'knowledge' implicit in art works may be thought superior to all other forms of knowledge, with the implication that it should therefore be taken as a paradigm for other intellectual aspirations. Such a claim could only be sustained by a demonstration that one way of utilizing experience is superior to others, a demonstration that is impossible to mount because of the lack of agreed criteria for 'measuring' the 'quality' of experience. (And vice-versa the same objection cripples any utilitarian claim that all experiences are equally valuable.) As I argue throughout, not only are the boundaries of art as a distinctive activity socially constructed in any particular context, but the criteria of worth which in part justify this distinctiveness are socially negotiated. If art can be seen to contain an account of the world, it is an account contingent upon a broader programme for organizing significant features of that world; and, as with all other ideological programmes, we can get some

leverage on the work they are designed to facilitate by investigating which
social group has formulated the programme and for which social audience.

I have argued that fictional performances embody knowledge of the
world that is not less true than other types of account and it is certainly
not less real as a mode of human action to produce and participate in the
performance. The central distinction between fiction and reality must
therefore concern the expectations of these participants. One way of
summarizing this distinction is to assert that fiction incorporates its own
reality whereas other accounts refer to a presumed reality. The use of
reference here harks back to the heuristic nature of technical accounts;
such accounts are implicitly situated *in* a world and are produced to aid
the accomplishment of that world. Fictional performances embody their
own terms of reference, while we participate in their accomplishment such
terms consitute a reality. Our expectations of a technical account are that
it will help to reveal further dimensions to our world, our expectations of
representation are that it will amplify that which we already understand
if not know.

The dialectic between art and society, that is the presumed lynch-pin
of 'social' accounts of representational meaning, is thus misconstrued if it
is interpreted as a dialectic between fictions and socio-physical reality. The
dialectic is rather within the productive enterprise of rendering a performance potent. The moments of the latter dialectic are productive
relations, the mode and milieu of presentation, and the significant uses
available to participants. More generally, I would like to argue that if we
can replace the conceptualization of society (form) acting as a backdrop
for individuals (content), with a conceptualization of society as a means of
negotiating individuality; then the question of determination in 'base—
superstructure' relationships disappears. The 'base' (that which makes
performances possible) necessarily informs the 'superstructure' (types of
fictional expression), because the latter is articulated through the former:
the content of narratives becomes expressible in different forms of context.
More immediately this approach has another implication: this is that if
the social dialectic of art is internal to its production and appreciation
then the vitality of representation is located in the process of *becoming
a product*, rather than in the vitality with which the means of representation are used to render a topic. 'The accomplished work is thus not the
work which exists in itself like a thing, but the work which reaches its
viewer and invites him to take up the gesture which created it' (Merleau-
Ponty 1974 p.48; the distinction is between an inscription and a
characterization). For example, the force of medieval cathedrals as asser-
tions of faith partly derives from the necessary technical accomplishments,
and partly derives from our knowledge of medieval Christianity as a
complement to other forms of feudal organization, and partly from the
scale of vision involved. Although cathedrals can be read iconographically,
and with great profit, their significance is primarily as an iconological

residue — a semi-permanent relic of incredible aspirations in a particular context (cf. Panofsky 1970 chap. 1 for the force of the distinction between iconography and iconology).

I claimed above that there are two ways in which it is useful to draw a distinction between how art as a way of knowing differs from other forms of knowledge. The second way I described as a concern with the relationships between forms of communication and that which is being communicated. If we see representational force as deriving from the process of becoming, being made, rather than from our contemplation of an object of accomplishment, then this has major implications for the relevance of a vocabulary of communication. In an important sense to speak of a form of knowledge is to speak a mode of communication: so that when we label the world, categorize it in a multiplicity of ways, we are rendering it malleable — opening it up so that others can share our grasp of significant features: 'What I have been suggesting here is that by describing events through particular terms and conventions of laguage, we have already explained the events, i.e. rendered them as an intelligible move in some game (ordering, obeying, murdering) of which our language speaks. So our descriptions constitute events' (Silverman 1975 p.22). It is impossible at the most fundamental level to draw a distinction between our knowledge and our ability articulate that knowledge, however imperfectly.

The common core of knowledge and speech can be described as a making-human. To know X and to speak X are humanizing in two ways. First, they both facilitate a utilization of experience, they imply a grasp of distinction between sign and signifier so that a distance is created. The brute flood of endless sensuality is broken up and the human capacity to reflect on self as with other topics of experience can be formulated in distinction to other animals' lack of consciousness (for a general discussion of the imposition of order see Bauman 1973). Secondly, signs are necessarily shared — to know a sign is to know another who shares that use of the sign concerned. Of course it is possible to develop individual mnemonics but their existence depends upon the prior acquisition of a conceptual vocabulary which is not personal. This is because the meaningfulness of a sign (concept etc.), depends upon its being used in accordance with appropriate rules, and if an infinite regress is to be avoided these rules must stem, eventually, from communal practice, rather than an individual's arbitrary decisions. It is in this sense that the idea of art as communication is most commonly put, that is that art extends our understanding of the world and is therefore a form of communication (for characteristic discussions see Hobsbawm 1970; Watson 1958). The difficulty with this approach is that easily leads to a concern with message transmission. To speak of knowledge as communication makes it sensible to attend to the amount of knowledge communicated. Information loss may be due to either 'noise' in the machinery of communication or to some feature of the recipients such that they fail to 'pick up' distinctive features of the message. I believe that a conceptualization of communication as a concern with messages is generally an impoverished approach, in relation to fictional performances it is particularly inappropriate.

It is fitting to refer a concern with message transmission as a consumerist ideology which, characteristically, has been far more influential in relation to popular entertainment than 'high' art. Although literary criticism has in general resisted positivist attempts to measure influence, very often being content with vague prescriptions of uses e.g. both Leavis and Hoggart; a consumerist ideology (the measurement of consequences), has been successful to the extent that it has interrelated with the distinction between art and society, (fiction and reality, base and superstructure), discussed in previous paragraphs. The implication of these remarks that a consumerist ideology has not been exclusively adopted by ideologists of consumerism is intentional; a common feature of vulgar 'Marxisms' is their concern with social needs and effects and an often totally arbitrary ascription of mystifying power to cultural forms allied with an inappropriate scientistic jargonizing. (See Williams 1977a for a cogent summary of consumerism in Marxist cultural writing.) The overlap between consumerism and an arbitrary distinction between fiction and reality can best be demonstrated by the relevance of the same alternative formulation to both mistakes. In both cases the knowledge inherent in representation is not a finite account, fictional performances embody a meaningful account through our participation in their formulation and development. I do not mean to suggest that through infinite participation one can render a performance infinitely meaningful — the organization of productive relationships does impose an important constraint on the significant uses possible. But it is necessary to stress that although a performance may contain a message this is not a necessary or even a central feature of representation, and therefore the communication in art is a communal recreating of a composition in performance not a measurement of performance effectiveness.

It will be apparent that once again I am locating the vital tension in representation between intentions and participation not appropriation of a completed object or product. I hope by this approach to provide some ground-work for the claim that the ideology of art as negotiable commodity in contemporary culture depends upon a reification of the object — an arbitrary abstraction into decorative form. I also hope to show that a 'cognitivist' approach to representational meaning is neither restricted to an empiricism of the real world nor to an idealism of disembodied form (cf. Scruton 1974 esp. part III). Performances are made through human actions in the context of other human actions and as such they bespeak social practices and aspirations, they help us to know what we are doing but the 'reality' of these actions is not a reflection of a real world: 'While it is doubtful that such complex programs directly "reveal" the culture in question, they do afford direct views of the way the culture *is presented* by and to its participants. And such "self-presentation" by and to some group is, we recall, the sort of paradox that "culture" is all about' (Boon 1973 p.19).

I have so far tried to bring out some features of art as a form of knowledge, as part of the more general enterprise of clarifying the sociology of culture. My reason for opening up theoretical issues is that one of my main intentions in this work is to find a way of talking about popular art which goes beyond the implicit paternalism of most accounts of audience taste. I believe that if we are ever to transcend motivational theories of collective choice we have to find a way of opening up the world that is being made through the production and appreciation of popular art. I have argued that it makes sense to see representational imagery as constituting a way of knowing the world, but the discussion of this claim has left two important points unclarified. The first concerns that which is known: are some things more worth knowing than others? The second is closely related and concerns qualities of knowledge; are some ways of knowing better than others? In both cases the connection that is being made is not between knowledge and reality but more between knowledge and truth; that which we know is not only an aspect of our experience, it is also an aspect which can be evaluated.

These points are important because they help to being out the distinction between truth as descriptive fidelity and truth as authenticity (that is the fidelity with which the author attempts to explore the implications of his audience's expectations). In the same way that art has been argued to articulate a distinctive mode of knowledge, so we can argue that a comparable connection can be made between art and truth: 'in so far as he communicates the image of his perception to his fellow men, the artist is morally responsible for it. . . . This means that society cannot be indifferent whether a given work of art inspires by its profound insight, whether it stirs to action, whether it soothes and refreshes, or whether, on the other hand, it opiates and disrupts. And it also means that the *aesthetic value* of a work of art must in some way be related to the effect it produces, not merely in its own time, but as long as it survives' (Klingender 1975 pp.8-9). The point being made here is a common feature of attacks on aestheticism: the work of art cannot be divorced from its social context and its meaning is centrally dependent upon its significance in that context. In as much as the sociologist starts from the presupposition that meaning is a socially constituted enterprise, sociological accounts of art are inextricably caught up with the truth or not of the material with which they are concerned. These remarks are an effective introduction to a functionalist theory of art (cf. Iser 1975), a position I modify in the course of the essay.

The field of popular art poses distinctive difficulties in this respect. In many ways what we understand as popular art has been defined by its lack of truth, in the sense that entertainment is mystifying, deflecting attention from significant features of experience. For some years this critique was formulated in terms of a debate over the culture of mass society (Jacobs 1961; McQuail 1969), and although this concern has become less fashionable in the last few years, the presumptions of mystifying power are still commonly made. (Examples of work which while trying to develop a political economy of ownership and control presumes effects are Murdoch and Golding 1974; 1977). The conventional response to the popular-art-as-opiate criticisms has been in terms of an attempted empirical refutation with all the consequent absurdities of attempts to measure alienation (cf. Chaney 1972 part 1), rather than a more serious concern with the reality that is being 'masked'. A second type of criticism of popular culture is that it denies authenticity by subverting audience expectations. The necessity to industrialize distribution so that a performance is as widely available as possible has been held to mean that any particular performance loses its uniqueness. The industrialization of multiple performances is likely to lead to the standardization of production procedures thus doing away with individual idiosyncrasies. And for the same reasons performances are likely to attempt to reproduce established successes rather than innovate new styles.

There are therefore two main senses in which popular art has been held to be failing to express truth: first, because of its ideological role in mass society it acts to dupe and mislead the gullible proletariat; and second, because of the nature of its production it is denied the possibility of expressing any personal understanding and is restricted to reproducing stereotypical versions of experience. There is a paradox here, and it is an important paradox, in that popular art is ostensibly closer to the 'real' world than other forms of fictional account. The very term popular denotes everyday acceptance and the entertainment we are thinking of seems both immersed in a self-evident world and to be predominately concerned with reproducing 'realistic' dramas of that world. Not only is popular art centrally concerned with meeting the canons of popular taste, and therefore implicit criteria of what is appropriate, in a hierarchical society what is identifiably 'of' the people is jealously guarded as something that has a private significance which cannot be appreciated on terms of conventional criticism and appreciation. Realism, with its dual connotations of knowledge and truth, therefore presents distinctive difficulties in relation to popular art, and if we are to take popular art seriously we have to go some way towards appreciating the paradoxes of realism.

In order to develop this argument we have to begin by exploring the peculiar salience of realism for aesthetic imagination in the nineteenth century. It is precisely because the massive industrialization of the nineteenth century involved such extensive recasting of forms of life for all social groups that reality came to be seen instrumentally rather than as a necessity. The fabrics of the social and physical orders were being restitched more or less consciously throughout the century and this was obviously a backcloth against which significant features of experience were being proposed as well as captured. A concern with the multiplicity of realities does not become a predominant characteristic either intellectually or imaginatively until the latter years of the century; realism and surrealism are themes developed in the next section. (For a rare and interesting attempt to look at some of the overlap between intellectual and imaginative concerns see Berger 1970 on Schutz and Musil; see also the excellent paper by Barbara Petrocci in which she observes that the character of urban heterogeneity led both Simmel and Musil to arrive at the identical conclusion: city life boils down to the habit of *putting mind over matter*' (1976 p.4) — a very interesting thesis in relation to the approach to realism I am about to develop.) The argument that realism is essentially the imaginative form for popular art in industrializing societies is therefore, at first, that the exigencies of making a new reality threw up such overriding topics that the attempt to capture them faithfully was automatic. A second argument that popular art is for certain essential reasons necessarily a realist genre will be developed after the first.

The Realist Impulse

The realist impulse is not used here to refer to a genre, more an implicit style. Of course there are periods in the history of each medium of expression when the predominant style of work can be called 'realist' as a descriptive label which usefully differentiates the work from other styles. An example would be the self-ascription of realism by individuals clustered around Courbet and Champfleury in mid-nineteenth-century France. The realist impulse does not solely refer to such moments; rather it refers to a persistent trend which underlies work in a wide variety of styles and which can be said to 'surface' more or less explicitly in the work of different groups at different times. The argument might be easier to grasp if we spoke of documentary aspirations rather than realist impulse. The continuity is that both terms signal an engagement with experience, a desire to know the world instead of aspiring to perfect an already given form.

Documentary expression is in practice as ambiguous a term as realism or any other. Stott (1973) demonstrates that the idea of documenting experience can be interpreted as providing documents, facts, which unselfconsciously record events from the standpoint of a participant rather an historian or writer of fiction, a classic example is a diary; or as a human record which attempts to reconstruct experience as it really was, for example Flaherty's attempt to capture the essence of Eskimo life in *'Nanook of the North'* (Stott 1973 part 1). The idea of documentary is therefore that in either sense it is providing an authentic account, it is a picture of the world which eschews artifice. The paradoxes of this aspiration are self-evident. First, the ability to record as well as merely participating requires the author to self-consciously distance himself from 'the action'. Artifice is introduced through recording procedures, whatever they are, in that distance is employed to get a purchase on significant features of experience so that others although not physically present can share it. Secondly, the documentary aspiration to reconstruct experience presumes a 'real' reality which can be known, it lies beyond or behind the surface patina of what has happened. This is paradoxical in that such an account is necessarily an interpretation, a persuasive version to which we might assent once it is available to us but which is not self-evidently there shared by all participants in the experience.

These paradoxes point to a distinction by now well established in the critical tradition. This is the distinction between naturalism and realism (cf. Lukacs 1963). Naturalism is a concern with surface detail, it is oriented towards reproducing the world as it is conventionally known; realism in contrast tries to go beyond surface phenomena to detect significant truths. Burke makes the same distinction in another and perhaps more telling way when he introduces the distinction between realism of detail and realism of structure (Burke 1972 chap. 2). The latter is more real because it situates any event or experience in an historical context of how it became so and a synchronic context of other significant features. It is in these ways that we come to appreciate the force of Williams's contention that realism is a normative judgement not a description of the world. The realist enterprise is implicitly looking to make a world as it should be rather than describe a world as it is (Williams 1961 part 2, chap. 7). In a more recent paper Williams (1977b) has developed the idea of a realist 'attitude' which he argues has three characteristic emphases: 'The secular, the contemporary and the socially extended'. These headings provide an appropriate bridge between documentary description and realist reconstruction.

These paragraphs have been written as an introduction to the claim that the realist impulse is essentially an epistemological quest; it is a search for 'better' knowledge and a dissatisfaction with the terms of conventional knowledge. To create and judge a form of life it is necessary to envisage other forms and other cultures. To return to a point made in previous chapters, there is an analogy between realism and ethnography; in the present context a comparative attitude encourages a concern with underlying form rather than surface content — and so innovators of abstraction could see themselves as the first true realists. Knowing other forms exist is insufficient, the artist has to see them as relevant possibilities for his own work. It has been suggested that in nineteenth-century Western Europe for the first time stylistic heterogeneity became an everyday occurence, work could be borrowed if a style was seen to be appropriate for a particular context (Vogt 1973). This was possible because the effect became the prime criterion in judging a work, the producer became conscious of the style of his work as a thing to be chosen — his choice is necessarily saying something about himself, about the context of the work and about users of his and other work in that context. It is against this background that I will suggest the following three reasons as being particularly important in promoting a climate for realist aspirations. First, the intellectual climate of secular scientism; secondly, the professionalism of production; and finally the felt flexibility of the social order.

The Industrial Revolution in any European country was never an identifiable set of events occuring within a specific time-period, it is more usefully understood as a coalescence and acceleration of a number of changes in different fields. An important feature of this climate of change was the acceptance of innovation, not just in technical advance but in related fields of thought and action. I think that the range of intellectual activity in the closing decades of the eighteenth century and opening decades of the nineteenth is best characterized as secular humanism (Klingender 1972). It seems to me that in relation to culture, this humanism gradually fractures into contrasting styles of aestheticism and cashbox aesthetics. What changed was the gradual proliferation of accepted styles of inquiry: the artist was forced to choose and justify both his topic and his manner of addressing that topic, leading inevitably to a concern with how that topic came to be formulated. The Romantic onslaught on Classical values had resulted in a profusion of subjects, but also meant that the world to be encompassed sometimes threatened to overflow the medium of narration — as in the apocalyptic adaptations of industrial imagery by painters like John Martin. The post-Classical freedom to include details of mundane experience grounded the dramatic narrative and facilitated a multiplicity of plot levels which did not have to be harmoniously arranged. In practice the use of detail in most Victorian painting is illustrative of preconceived attitudes and the picture becomes a text to be read for the implications of clues: 'The Victorian paintings can only produce a much more limited response — instead of fascinatingly involving us in the mystery and uncertainty of personality, they invite us to indulge a comfortable disapproval or moralizing sympathy' (Conrad 1973 p.59).

We can clarify this point by briefly noting some of the shifts in contemporary usage of concepts of culture and civilization. The self-confident homogeneous cultural universe of eighteenth-century leisured society was disrupted by the gradual development of contradictory uses of culture and civilization. The latter term was gradually adopted, reaching its full flowering in 1851, as a descriptive term for the rational, technical efficiency of industrialist capitalist entrepreneurs. The material tangibility of mechanical artefacts was an inescapable demonstration of civilization's superiority. In contrast culture came to be used as a synonym for the inviolable domain of the spirit; romanticism survived through maintaining a self-conscious aesthetic distance from the bruising demands of civilized efficiency. Coexisting with these uses was another pair of contrasts in which culture was used as a descriptive term to capture the form of life of strange societies both foreign primitive peoples and indigenous proletarian masses; while in contrast civilization referred to the achievements of a moral education in a growing number of public schools. These contrasts have survived throughout this century and still serve as sources of confusion in cultural debate. They can be summarized as different attempts to formulate a coherent attitude to the relationship between knowledge and experience.

Precisely because the physical world as a set of taken-for-granted constraints on possible action was dissolving through the new social relationships engendered by machines, the objects of inquiry could not be presumed. Instead the manner of intellectual reflection implied possible topics. For example, a concern with stages of social evolution as in the work of Comte and Saint-Simon presumes the variability of social order and the possibility of producing criteria to justify one choice rather than another. Similarly, the depiction of peasants as other than sentimentalized 'natural' men by Courbet was profoundly shocking in that it presumes the topic of class differences and the possibility of producing criteria to change those differences (cf. Clarke 1973). It is in the transformation of relationship between an author and his audience that one can look for a distinction between the shift of perspective involved in Renaissance humanism and that of nineteenth-century realism. The former was principally a change in means of addressing a topic although in time it became part of a general change in type of topic addressed, the latter was more concerned with the grounds upon which topics were accepted as appropriate. The types of knowledge being sought helped to constitute the type of enquiry pursued and thereby the form of art made.

The implication of this argument concerning the significance of different types of fictional enquiry is that it becomes possible to criticize certain types of authorship for being based on bad faith or being inauthentic. For example, it is apparent that the forms of popular sentimentalism generally known as socialist realism are inauthentic through their persistent refusal to explore the grounds of their own narrative stance. The consequence of this 'silence' is fictional idealism rather than materialism. In this particular case there are bureaucratic agencies which exist to maintain a particular relationship between author and audience, and reify certain conceptualizations of fictional relationships to reality. In social circumstances in which the performance is centrally valued as a commercial commodity, stylistic heterogeneity is an inevitable concomitant of instrumental attitudes, in that the manner of addressing reality will change with shifts in conceptions of different work for different contexts. This has in turn two further consequences which constitute our second reason of professionalism of production. The first consequence is that producers will come to pride themselves on their ability to master a range of styles, a catalogue of dialects from which they choose as they think fit (or what they think they can get away with). The second is that a hierarchy of styles in terms of personal authenticity becomes possible. This hierarchy may be structured in relation to an individual, so that only when he is doing X style is he truly expressing himself; or in relation to the styles of a period or country, for example Pre-Raphaelite criticisms of the inauthenticity of cashbox aesthetics at that time. Both consequences will tend to mean that producers come to introduce distinctions within and between those audiences who can 'really' appreciate the true worth of performances.

The most widely appreciated version of the audience as a possible threat is the development of a bohemia, not in the raffish 'wild-oats' style of early nineteenth century best preserved in light opera, but as a cultural ghetto in which outsiders become insiders and knowledge becomes personal understanding (see Poggioli 1968; see also the very interesting paper by Sanguineti, 1973, on the paradoxical attempt to escape commercialism at the heart of every avant-garde). The bohemia(n) in this sense is an invention of the last hundred years and represents an attempt to preserve a private grasp of authentic expression. Such a search for authenticity entails the artist making a reality rather than copying it. In relation to pictorial display Nochlin (1971) has suggested that the invention of the camera accelerated moves towards subjectivity because of the impossibility of being 'better' than a camera, but the camera was also welcomed as an aide to capturing certain fragments of the passing world. It was copied structurally not internally, that is its way of making an image was used not the content of that image. If the audience is not a threat because it will emasculate the author, there may be a grudging compromise in which those producers who define their work purely within 'professional' criteria – giving the public what they want – are forced to accept public conceptions as constituting the reality of their work. Within the constraints of the productive organization and public conceptions of appropriate performance they provide work which is technically excellent and necessarily reinforces the implicit account of such a world in which such performances are non-problematic dramatic narratives.

Whichever of these extremes, bohemianism or technical excellence, is the career choice of the young entrant to popular art production, there is a common ground of respect for the work. This is interestingly complemented by the process in which members of different audiences will come to concentrate their attention on the performance as authors become anonymous employees of large organizations. For both the producers and audiences the work is something apart from themselves — it has an autonomy as something potentially admirable seemingly in its own right. In one sense the equation of sincerity with conscientiousness can be taken to mean that reality is painfully being constructed through aesthetic fabrication: 'Such technique is indeed a conquest — a victory over nature, comparable with the effort of science to control the elements, or with that of the historical novel to gain intellectual control of the past' (Conrad 1973 p.128; see also Murdoch 1975). Another aspect of labour constituting art is the utopian naturalism of much popular culture. Although I am arguing that there is a key relationship between fiction and reality in popular experience, realism in popular art is less likely to be an explicit engagement with the boundaries of conventional forms of knowledge, than an exploration of romantic or exciting or spectacular or intriguing or sentimental etc., alternatives to everyday experience. Such utopias have to be comprehensible and possible, i.e. they need a realism of detail to sustain the narrative but they usually lack a realism of structure — set in the terms of genre forms which stereotype narrative resolution. Popular art tends to be naturalistic except that its narratives are alternatives, they postulate a world other than the everyday, which has been carefully constructed and which is inherently extraordinary. The performance invites our wonder and admiration because it spectacularly shows up the arbitrary basis of distinctions between the real and the surreal.

The central reason why alternative types of story-telling are potentially subversive of conventional conceptions of the real is that a spectre haunted the industrial social order. Industrialization necessitated the development of enormous property-less urban labouring masses. These classes not only changed the existing social order but have posed a continual threat to succeeding versions of ordered society. This is both because of the frequently appalling conditions in which labourers were expected to work and live, and because of their continuing resentment of being used as a labour resource on a par with other raw materials. The perceived instability of the social order is a topic I have discussed more fully in the previous chapter. In this chapter I want to emphasize the distinctive tensions involved in fictional representations which involve realistic performances as ourselves for ourselves. Conrad has pointed out that a common solution for Victorian artists was to push the subject of the work back in time, so that it could be framed by nostalgia and idealization: 'Fildes was horrified when in 1908 a German photogravurist suggested that his Venetian subject *The Devotee* should be retitled *Lancashire Lassie,* because factory girls also wore shawls over their heads: the picture's sentiment depended on its not possessing that topical relevance the German wished to give it' (op. cit. p.188). More generally it seems that the tensions of social commentary could to some extent be neutralized by swamping a realism of detail in suffocating genre sentiments which preserved the vicarious distance of fictional platitudes.

If some such strategy of neutralization is not followed then a concern with artistic responsibility is likely to lead the author to identify his narrative viewpoint with that of the subjects of his work. Such a dissolution of the boundaries between artist and entertainer has radical implications for the status of the fiction being enacted — the thrust of realism becomes inverted and the performance becomes reality. The subordination of the artist to his work (i.e. he becomes indistinguishable from the craftsman and/or the entertainer) entails only a short step to the people being the work. Thus the documentary movement in the thirties made 'real' people the topic and to some extent attempted to derive a style which was authentic to the topic (see Barnouw 1974). Although this process is radical in regard to the presuppositions of fictional boundaries, it is not necessarily radical in its social or political implications. Stott has pointed out the functional role of some documentaries: 'This is the reason the human documents in the news are read: they offer safe exercise for the reader's feelings; they test — but gently — his emotional competence to live in the great world that day. . . . And the answer is always yes. The reader cannot lose. . . . He can face up to them [human documents] as he cannot be sure he will always face up to his own life, because they treat of someone else's' (Stott 1973 pp.16-7). More interestingly Ray (1971) has suggested that the social documentaries carried out by Mass Observation in Britain were an extension of the surrealist attempt to let the unconscious hand dictate the pen — in this case a collective hand. The immediate relevance of this observation is that the model for this type of collective biography was the everyday ethnography of newspapers and films.

A second aspect of the perceived fragility of the social order is the salience of popular imagery to fictional expression, and the ways in which the social realities this imagery was part of could be adapted and transformed in making narrative forms more acceptably consonant with contemporary ideologies. In Barbara Hardy's study of 'the narrative imagination' she is concerned with the interweaving of narrative devices from everyday experience into more self-conscious fictions: 'great comic novelists who are sufficiently assured of their virtuosity to be able to fool about with it, brilliant clowns who feign clumsiness, naivete, uncertainty or ineptness in order to make quite certain that we don't mistake something that looks easy for something that is easy' (Hardy 1975 p.9). We can reread such literary constructions in order to see the uses to which narrative devices have been put. To take a particularly significant example, the status of gossip in a community may act as a medium of collective self-interest which is 'in the main kindly'. The fragility of the community as a point of reference for nineteenth-century depictions of social experience perhaps explains the absence from novels of 'communal kindliness': 'The game of whispers seems impelled towards malignancy by its very imperfect communication. Gossip is a form of joint egging-on, whose moments of kindliness gloss over, license, or prop-up unworthier speculations' (*op. cit.* p.130; see also the discussion in Williams 1973). Another example is provided by Kinser and Kleinman's (1969) investigation of popular imagery in both formulating and articulating national consciousness in Germany in the first half of this century. The authors suggest that mythic themes and forms persist in a culture at a number of 'levels' of quality and consciousness, for example political rhetoric, cartoons, postcards and architecture. This vocabulary of imagery helps to structure conventional understanding of communal identity in that culture. In the particular example of twentieth-century Germany there was a fairly explicit attempt to realize political practices derived from these themes, not to make politics popular but to structure politics with popular imagery.

I cannot sustain, nor do I wish to, an argument that the realist impulse is manifested in art in industrial societies and in no others (for some random discussion of realism in non-industrial contexts see Watson 1974 part 2; Pollitt 1972 chap. 3). Nor can I sustain an argument that all performances in industrial societies should be interpreted as 'really' realist, this would be patently absurd. Suitably qualified therefore, my argument is that realism is curiously salient for art in industrial societies in ways that are not so salient for other social contexts. In the preceeding pages I have given some reasons why this argument seems to both sustainable and worth sustaining. It will be noticed, however, that my approach so far has been contextual in that I have talked about the inter-relationships between performances and context as a way of explicating the stance of a performance to that context. What has been missing has been any concern with the implications of industrialization for the production of performances as work. To conclude this section I shall therefore briefly discuss some features of the work of art in the age of mechanical reproduction. The use of this phrase signals that my account will mainly consist of a reading of some essays by Walter Benjamin.

My perspective has been organized around the argument that a performance does not get its identity from a set of distinctive features which together comprise its form and content. Rather its identity is a mediation between such features, the effective physical and socio-cultural context in which the performance is made and the conceptual frameworks with which audiences interpret the performance. Benjamin suggests that when this mediation is concerned with the unique existence of a performance it is oriented towards the 'authenticity of a thing [which] is the essence of all that is transmissible from its beginning, ranging from its substantive duration to its testimony to the history which it has experienced' (1970 p.223). Such authenticity derives from the personal texture of the work in the context of relevant traditions reinforced by a concept of distance: 'What is aura? A peculiar web of space and time: the unique manifestation of a distance, however near it may be' (Benjamin 1972 p.20). The idea of distancing as a characteristic feature of art works is not of course peculiar to Benjamin: 'The difference between the reality of the audience and the unreality of the stage is the "aesthetic distance" which sanctions the conventional signals and percepts of the performance. It is this that is the essential source of the play's style' (Styan 1975 p.69); but his use of it as a version of quasi-ritualized abstraction from everyday life helps to fill out his more generalized concept of the aura of art works: 'that which withers in the age of mechanical reproduction is the aura of the work of art' (Benjamin 1970 p.223).

To the extent that the aura is a more sophisticated version of a concept of identity, Benjamin's thesis is that the identity of performances dies when they are endlessly reproduced. Before I go on to expand this claim I should note in passing that I am using reproduction in rather a distinctive sense here. I am not concerned with the existence of copies of performances, these have always existed and presumably the only change in our recent history is that technological improvements facilitate more 'accurate' copies. Serial reproduction of performances refers to situations where there is no qualitative or possibly even physical distinction between the original and copies, where, that is, the performance is potentially simultaneously available to infinite audiences. Benjamin makes this point clearly and the examples he stresses, photography and film, are both clear illustrations of the strong sense of reproduction. It is interesting to note in this context that the difficulty of distinguishing between compositions and performances for these media poses enormous problems for processes of artistic legitimation, such as the museumization and canonization of authors (for two very different discussions of this point see Berger 1972; Christopherson 1974).

This conceptualization of serial reproduction clearly makes identity very problematic. The mediations between the performance and its context are as potentially infinite as the number of audiences, and therefore no one mode of interaction can be claimed to be intrinsically more rewarding than any other. Thus the decay of aura is part of a process of the democratization of objects and experience. A sense of the 'universal equality of things' means that the maker of performances is forced to immerse himself in the world he is commenting upon. His distinctive techniques justify themselves because they presume a neutrality in their use, they are designed to provide the best possible use of themselves rather than the best possible expression of the producer's 'vision'. In brief, the loss of aura means the loss of distance so that topics are equivalent and equally transitory, and therefore depicting the world is commiting the producer to an account of the world more than to an account of himself: 'To an ever greater degree the work of art reproduced becomes the work of art designed for reproducibility. . . . But the instant the criterion of authenticity ceases to be applicable to artistic production, the total function of art is reversed. Instead of being based on ritual, it begins to be based on another practice — politics' (1970 p.226).

The implicit suggestion in the previous paragraph is that the medium comes to supplant the producer as the ideological rationale for the meaning of the work. To put this another way, Benjamin seems to be arguing that when a work of art had a distinctive identity (aura), the meaning of the work was very directly related to the intentions of the producer in his productive context. The qualitative shift from ritual to use, reproducibility, involves a shift from intentions to uses — uses which are sold in competition with other commodities in the market-place of diversions.

The process through which the facility of reproducibility fundamentally changes the significance of the author is reinforced by comparable shifts in the position of the audience. Because the performance is dependent upon technological instruments for reproduction and these instruments are not bound by human senses, the means come to supplant the audience as the 'object' of the performance and the audience identifies with the means more than the performer: 'The audience's identification with the actor is really an identification with the camera. . . . The aura which, on the stage, emanates from Macbeth, cannot be separated by the spectators from that of the actor. However, the singularity of the shot in the studio is that the camera is substituted for the public. Consequently, the aura that envelops the actor vanishes, and with it the aura of the figure he portrays' (1970 pp.230-1).

It is in this way that we are led to the most important point that the centrality of the medium, usurping the autonomy of producer and audience, means that *the medium is necessarily making a world rather than reflecting one*. The loss of distance means that the performance is incorporated in its own world, an incorporation expressed and articulated through the features of technological manufacture which infinitely reproducible performances necessitate. To elucidate this point Benjamin uses as a long analogy the contrast between a magician and a surgeon, in order to illustrate the difference between a painter and a cameraman: 'Magician and surgeon compare to painter and cameraman. The painter maintains in his work a natural distance from reality, the cameraman penetrates deeply into its web. There is a tremendous difference between the pictures they obtain. That of the painter is a total one, that of the cameraman consists of multiple fragments *which are assembled under a new law*. Thus for contemporary man the representation of reality by the film is incomparably more significant than that of the painter' (1970 pp.235-6).

The consequence of this thesis is that we realise that the central issue in serial reproduction is not how 'authentic' a performance is (if by authentic we mean faithful to an objective reality), but the criteria by which reality is assembled within a performance (that is an understanding of authenticity which turns on consciousness of social implications). Precisely because realism is being assembled, it is being constituted in a performance; it cannot be judged by refering to a correspondence with an 'external' world but must be judged by how the processes of assembling are being done, — by the aspirations for the performance of those engaged in its work: 'The crucial point, therefore, is that a writer's production must have the character of a model: it must be able to instruct other writers in their production and, secondly, it must be able to place an improved apparatus at their disposal. This apparatus will be the better, the more consumers it brings in contact with the production process — in short, the more readers or spectators it turns into collaborators' (1973 p.98). This injunction should not be read as a vulgar command to control the commanding heights of productive organization — shuffling managerial elites does nothing for the rules by which we assemble fragments of experience; the ramifications of making realistic performances go beyond reading messages to sensing social forms in which such messages become possible. The logic of this analysis is that the production of performances need not be restricted to exceptionally gifted individuals, indeed the technological breadth of the performance encompasses the world so that: 'Authority to write is no longer founded in a specialist training but in a polytechnical one, and so becomes common property' (1973 p.90). Authoritative interpretations are not sustainable because there is no authority in the text but power derives from the uses which a text may facilitate. To question the authority of distinctions between production and reception is to envisage the possibility of the world consciously being made instead of experienced, thus a possible epigraph for the chapter: 'The adjustment of reality to the masses and of the masses to reality is a process of unlimited scope, as much for thinking as for perception' (1970 p.225).

In conclusion I shall summarize some of the main points made and indicate their relevance to the production of fictional realism. The first is that a performance cannot sustain its own authority as a unique piece of work when it exists as it is reproduced and not as it is. Therefore its apart-ness from the real world, either as a venerated object or as a privileged experience, is undercut; it is part of the multiple fragments of possible experience which constitute our style of life. The performance is fictional because the narrative is subject to our whim, when we lose control of our narratives reality is written for us instead of by us and thus becomes an instrumental fiction. The second is that as serial reproduction facilitates endless simultaneous presentation the concept of audience becomes an infinitely more complex idea. (In any particular medium there will be technological constraints on why endless simultaneous presentation is not possible, but the extension of cheap private receivers into every medium will shortly render this a technical possibility.) Instead of an audience being those who attend a performance, the audience must include many different degrees and styles of attention. In this sense what it means to be a mem-ber of an audience is something that is articulated in each particular membership and is not given any essential characteristics. Thirdly, I have emphasized the impossibility of an artist claiming a privileged status if there is no essential authority to his work. Thus distinctions between artist, craftsman and entertainer become self-evidently arbitrary judgements and many authors exploit this ambivalence to parody their own pretensions e.g. Graham Greene, Andy Warhol and Alfred Hitchcock.

A history of European cultural production would have to include an account of how the emergence of art as a self-conscious activity was dependent upon artists as a group becoming conscious of distinctive features of their work, although their work remained 'given' by a geographic, temporal and cultural location. The argument being formulated in this section is that serial reproduction led to style becoming self-conscious; how a performance is done becomes a conscious choice. In part this is because the multitude of audiences requires a decision on for whom one writes (cf. Sartre 1962 for an explicit attempt to write out the implications of posing that question), and in part because in Benjamin's terms writing is a model which can include the audience as collaborators — whether or not to use this facility always involves a decision (in the terms of the previous chapter the recognition of a multitude of publics makes serial thought inherently ideological). This is why performances in an era of serial reproduction are engaged in a making of reality through the implicit social order they advocate. This is the real force of technological innovation that McLuhan summarized as medium rather than message. It is characteristic of his romantic reaction that he only understood his insight to mean that technology promotes social forms rather than that the adjustment of reality to our purposes is articulated through social forms which require shifting conceptions of means and medium. The reconsideration of the position of the author in relation to public and audience means that a presumed reality in the social order is always tendentious.

Realism and Modernism

A discussion which concentrates on the relationship between fictional experience and the real world might be expected to be oriented towards undercutting the pretensions of authors, to show how their work is parasitic on events and processes beyond their control. In practice I have tried to show how a concern with realism is likely to lead to a celebration of fictionality. By this I mean an emphasis upon the distinctiveness of fictional representations and the significance of different modes of fictional expression for the community in which such stories are told. A concern with the boundaries of fiction and the attitudes adopted towards real resources, — in these ways the status of cultural forms as they interrelate with other cultural practices in the community becomes more apparent. This type of inquiry is particularly important for studies of popular culture because the very anonymity of most performances is likely to encourage a feeling that styles are self-evident and a natural consequence of contemporary facilities. I have tried to show that in practice the presuppositions of story-telling as an elaboration of reality structure the 'realism' of such stories. I have organized this approach around a number of view-points, one is the form of knowledge, the style of speech that symbolic representation presumes, another derives from the socio-institutional contexts in which this style has been articulated in urban-industrial societies, and a third is concerned with the implications of a performance being manufactured endlessly for fictional distance. From each of these viewpoints the 'realness' of fictional work is a central dimension of why the performance has seemed to be saying something. Thus we come to the final paradox of realist aspirations that the most distinctive feature of art in the twentieth century has been a celebration of fictionality that has consisted of a refusal to correspond to the constraints of conventional accounts of reality.

It may be appropriate to refer to this process as a move to abstraction, and if so we can begin to consider some of the senses in which the characterization is justified. First, there has been less attempt to disguise the fictional character of a performance. Thus if a pictorial display is limited to two-dimensional representation then this limitation becomes a central feature of the display attempted (there are characteristic discussions of this point in relation to types of modernism in Golding 1959 and Nash 1974). Similarly, film and theatre performances have tended to explore the artificiality of the manner of their own presentation, for example Brecht and Fellini, as a device for asserting a distinctive stance. Secondly, the conventional expectation for the content of a performance is that it can be read as a dramatic narrative — there is a story which unfolds through time. This expectation has been continually ruptured in that in many media content has shifted from narrative to how a comprehensible narrative might be reached; Godard's remark about his films having a beginning, middle and end but not necessarily in that order is a well-known exemplification of this point. An inevitable consequence of this change is that the narrator, as the medium of relevance, rather than the author assumes a central position. Thirdly, the boundaries of media have been broken in many different types of performance. By boundaries I mean the conventional physical form in which the performance is cast, for example theatrical performances on the street rather than on a stage; or pictorial displays which are 'on' natural forms rather on a framed canvas; or literary work which randomly agglomerates text on separate sheets rather than being presented as a bound sequential set of pages. The distinctiveness of a performance in all these cases therefore comes to depend on conventions of the work, instead of the work being based on conventions of naturalism. Thus it is more difficult to know how to follow, to know how to read.

In all these various ways twentieth-century art has come to seem more difficult, more abstract because it is less possible to see these works as examples of 'real' art. (The fact that it is conventional to equate abstraction with difficulty is all the more surprising when we bear in mind that members of less 'sophisticated' societies do not find non-representational imagery problematic. This might suggest that criteria of representational fidelity in our culture serve an important ritual function.) A related criticism of modernism concentrates upon the lack of coherence, the savage juxtapositions which suggest the fragmented vision of hallucination rather than the calm reflection of academic science. Lukacs, writing with ascetic distaste for decadence, has argued that the consequence of modernism is that: 'Distortion becomes the normal condition of human existence; the proper study, the formative principle, of art and literature' (1963 p.33). At this point I do not want to become embroiled in an assessment of the progressive possibilities of modernism (I return to some aspects of this discussion in the concluding chapter), but I do want to bring out the parallels between the explorations of the boundaries of normality and the construction of reality. The paradox that a reconsideration of the presuppositions of narrative form such that such forms could more closely conform to the dynamics of practical experience, should lead to the solipsistic uncertainties of modernism may at first seem startling. But the logic of this relationship is in fact inherent in all the points that have been made so far. The connection between aesthetic self-consciousness and the arbitrary status of reality is a common concern with the forms through which experience and expression are possible. It is because the investigation of routine that is involved in realism leads to a consideration of the constitutive significance of social forms that *Ulysses* is the most intensive exploration of the mundane. The contrast to such formalism is a persistent romanticism which explores phenomenal sensuality rather than cognitive response.

The burden of this argument would seem to be that the painfully erected claims for realism *vis-à-vis* art in industrial society are being undercut. This would, however, be a misunderstanding. My point is that the rethinking of fictionality involved in what I have called the move to abstraction is the best demonstration of the realist impulse. This seeming paradox is not new and to some extent it is implicit in the conceptions of what producers thought their work involved, see for example some of the uses of realism such as Gabo and Pevsner's 'Realistic Manifesto' in Bann (1974); see also the rationale for Nash's remark that: 'The explanations were various but there was general agreement on one thing: that the Cubists were realists' (Nash 1974 p.23). More importantly, I claimed above that the realist impulse was essentially an epistemological quest, it stems from a desire to know the world through perfecting a given form: 'Pure reality can only be established through *pure* plastics. In its essential expression, pure plastics is unconditioned by subjective feelings and conceptions . . . particularities of form and natural colour evoke subjective states of feeling which obscure *pure reality*. To create pure reality plastically, it is necessary to reduce natural forms to the *constant elements* of form and natural colour to *primary colour*' (Mondrian quoted in Higgins 1973 p.2). It is because art as a way of knowing is a distinct engagement with experience that it becomes pointless to attempt to assess the realism (accuracy? authenticity?), of a performance by its correspondence to another way of knowing (form of speech). Instead realism becomes a desire to recollect the grounds through which that way of knowing becomes a considered, serious rather than frivolous form of speech: 'Essentially what speech *is* is a display, a making reference to an achievement, a way of showing itself as a thinking relation to a language as a speaking that hears' (Blum 1974 p.258).

I think it important at this point to emphasize that the move to abstraction is not specifically restricted to 'high' art. There are two aspects of this claim: first, a distinction between high and popular art based on one being representational and the other not is unsustainable; and secondly, many of the features which non-representational art aspires to develop are taken from forms of popular art. The distinction is not sustainable because it presumes an arbitrary classification of non-representational work as non-popular, whereas a lot of popular work is couched in terms of genres which are highly stylized but which utilize 'realistic' details. (An interesting book in this context which highlights many of these issues in relation to a particularly challenging medium, the cinema, is Armes\1974.) Examples of non-representational performances which take imagery and/or narrative forms from popular art are the use of comic-book iconography in paintings and films; and 'political' drama (*Tendenzliteratur*) in which details of everyday experience are used to demystify the meanings of taken-for-granted presuppositions.

An argument that the realist impulse in contemporary art has been transformed into the self-consciousness of modernism is not so controversial if it is confined to acknowledged innovators and radicals who found the constraints of naturalism restricting. It is, however, considerably more controversial if the same argument is applied to popular culture where innovations are likely to be concentrated at the level of technical expertise rather than transforming genres. And yet if we turn to examples of distinctive genres we find that even the most utopian forms of entertainment continually pose problems of appropriate narrative structure. The musical is a genre in which the requirement of realism seems at first sight most inappropriate, the cross-cutting dialogue, song and dance is self-evidently artifice unconstrained by fidelity to natural events. (Although it should be noted that the combination of the same elements can constitute a revolutionary performance which is realistic in a sense which similarly transcends the constraints of everyday experience — see the second part of Chapter Four.) In practice, however, those engaged in staging a musical are faced with problems of handling the transitions between different types of activity and the fact that the overall conjunction is unrealistic does not mean that the constituent elements do not have to be coherent. Attempts to integrate these diverse narrative elements are likely to lead to formal innovations which at first seem surrealistic and certainly very modernistic (see the interview with Stanley Donen in (Hillier 1977) for some remarks relevant to this point). The implication of this argument is that we ought to reconsider the distinction between realism of detail and realism of structure which has been used in this chapter. By realism of detail we ought to include narrative comprehensibility — a reasonableness of plot progression — but which certainly has structural implications. The consequence is that there seem good reasons for using the concept of narrative at two levels. The first is a coherent story and at this level realism relates to a correspondence between the conventions of story-telling in different social circumstances. The second level is the norms of relationships envisaged by the working out of the plot, and at this level realism relates to what I have called authenticity — a recognition of the responsibility of social implications. It is in this latter sense that the modernism of popular art is rarely realist, although the reasons for this are not inherent in populism but derive from the productive organizations which manufacture and distribute popular cultural performances in our society.

There is another aspect to the relationship between popular experience and realism which should be considered at this point. This is the connotation of popular in which it is used as a contrast to sophisticated. Thus work which is produced by amateurs for the enjoyment of themselves and their friends is often called popular or naive or primitive. One of the most interesting traditions of art-work produced under this heading is that of those painters who work outside the conventional institutions of artistic legitimation and reward (e.g. Cardinal 1974). This disparate collection of 'primitives' is relevant to our discussion at this point because their work is usually obsessively realistic, if by that term we mean the details are observed and faithfully recorded. Their work is unrealistic and indeed strikes the conventional viewer as primitive or surrealistic because the details are amalgamated in ways which override conventions of structure and scale and relevance: 'Thus we receive an exaggerated clarity, a more than real exactitude, in the attempt to achieve a palpable, graspable reality, yet this escapes willy-nilly into a Surrealist sphere, where everything becomes concrete and dreamlike at the same time, where everything has an equal value in the order of things. The view-point of the Naive is to have none, to be not aware of having to choose' (Hess 1975 p.95). Such a cavalier attitude to convention is of course one of the features of primitive work most admired by academically trained artists, so that their stance becomes a model for sophistication. This type of copying is, however, misplaced in that it accepts naivety at face value — it is to treat primitivism as a 'primary' natural vision rather than a perspective ignorant of critical consciousness. This type of popular art is in practice more akin to folk-cultural practices, it has yet to escape the instrumentalism of responding to the details of the fictionalized object; it has yet to acquire the confidence to be realistic in its own right.

I have been trying to deal with one of the main difficulties that my account has to face. If I argue that a concern with realism, the realist impulse, is the central dynamic of fictional representations in industrial societies then I trip over the fact that the predominant trend in media of expression in this century has been a shift towards abstraction — a climate

I have characterized as modernist. I have tried to indicate some reasons why realism is a confusing concept in this respect and why some authors have quite reasonably referred to their non-representational performances as realist. In relation to popular culture I have argued that the distinction between modernism and realism is not necessarily one of style but that realist authenticity involves more than a coherent narrative structure. Briefly, realism can be summarized as a consciousness of structuring which may require an ostensibly incoherent narrative form. I will attempt to clarify this thesis through taking up some aspects of the parallels between performances and forms of speech. In the previous paragraph I noted that as a performance is a way of knowing, reporting experience, it is a form of speech comparable with other modes of storytelling. In practice of course a performance is a discourse because it is not a monologue but a combination of discourses which are internally linked. For example every performance implies a narrator who may be a specific character or an idealized viewpoint, such as the unspoken 'I' of the novelist writing in the third person, or just the stance of the medium. In the case of the cinema the camera often acts as narrator giving the juxtaposition of new scenes an intelligibility which is not articulated.

The discourse of narrative is complemented by the discourse of the ostensible 'action', the story being told, which may itself be complemented by further discourses which are the dialogue of the fictional characters within the story. The knowledge of the performance is therefore grasped through the compatability of multiple discourses within the text, but as MacCabe (1974 p.9) points out: 'Whereas other discourses within the text are considered as material open to reinterpretation, the narrative discourse simply allows reality to appear and denies its own status as articulation'. Our conceptual vocabulary for this type of analysis can very easily become overloaded by distinctions and new terms, but it may help to specify some of the terms being used here more precisely. If we keep the term narrative discourse as a general heading for all the elements of the 'telling', then this discourse will consist of two types of constituent: 'The *diegesis,* narrative content or signified, is "what is being told", . . . *Narration* designates *HOW* the discourse is being produced, the process itself' (Hanet 1974 p.18). This distinction facilitates a further distinction which helps us to understand the aspiration of realism as fidelity. This latter distinction is that between the diegesis, as that represented, and the pro-filmic events as those events available to be represented. Not only does documentary aspire to achieve a complete union between the diegesis and the pro-filmic event, it also aspires to minimize the discrepancy between what would have happened had nobody taken any interest and what actually happened — the pro-filmic event (Vaughan 1976).

If the realist aspiration is to provide a performance which isomorphically mirrors events as they would have been then the aspiration is for work which is accurate at each of the levels of discourse; but this is of

course logically impossible because narrative discourse presumes itself
as an unexplicated resource through which the grounds of reality are un-
problematically apprehended. At its crudest the realist aspiration implies
that the only problem with reality is to go and see it, and, as MacCabe
once more points out, this in turn means that classic realism cannot see
the real as contradictory nor can classic realism encompass reality being
problematic for any audience. Even if we turn to more sophisticated
versions of composing reality, perhaps through a method of representational montage, these problems cannot be avoided: 'What Eisenstein
ignores is that the method of representation (the language: verbal or
cinematic) determines in its structural activity (the oppositions which
can be articulated) both the places where the object "appears" and the
"point" from which the object is seen' (MacCabe op. cit. pp.14-5; two
other papers which have looked interestingly at some of the problems
of 'being realistic' particularly in relation to film and photography are
Tudor 1972; and Willemen 1972). In arguing that a method of representation necessarily structures that which is depicted MacCabe is making a
point that has been reiterated through out this chapter in my recurrent
stress on fiction as making real. If the realist aspiration is conceived to be
a more or less successful copy of a world then the paradoxical inadequacies
of the idea will eventually become apparent, but if the process of structuring *is* the achievement, if it is a way of speaking that continually refers
to the language of which it is an exemplification then realist aspirations
will render the reading subject a co-locuter not just a listener.

There is another way I can illustrate the problems with literal realism.
This is the argument that a performance which aspires to be literally
faithful to the world as it is has to be consistent with the facts of the
fictionalized object. By facts of the fictionalized object I do not
just mean the phenomenal features of that object, but the structures of
space and time in which those facts are located. Thus a two-dimensional
picture in order to be realistic has to be a representation of a two-
dimensional subject, i.e. another representation: 'Such paintings are
pictures of themselves rather than pictures of things' (Battcock 1975
p.xxix). It is in this sense that we can argue that actors representing the
sexual act do not do it more realistically when they actually copulate on
the stage but when the privacy of their interaction is potentially invadable.
The paradox is that the only representations which are literally realistic in
this sense are icons of supernatural deities who do not have physical
correlates. Such representations, often described as fantastic or surreal,
may be to all intents and purposes effectively literally realistic. The
consequence of this analysis is that representation is necessarily selective —
it is a persuasive version of significant features of that which is being
represented. If we respond to this version at the level of content we are
concerned with the description available in the representation; we are trying to correlate externally two sets of information and decide whether the

match is appropriate. The alternative is to be concerned with the way the representation is put together — how the narrative is constructed. From this perspective we cannot correlate but have to contrast the point of view which gives coherence to the story with the point of view of each of us as a member of the audience for such a story. A narrative analysis is there-fore an attempt to lay bare the mechanisms by which the fictional experience has come to seem reasonably accomplished. An analysis which does not have to be a critical exegesis but can be an element in the narration: 'A work of art, understood dynamically, is just this process of arranging images in the feelings and mind of the spectator. It is this that constitutes the peculiarity of a truly vital work of art and distinguishes it from a lifeless one, in which the spectator receives the represented result of a given consummated process of creation, instead of being drawn into the process as it occurs' (Eisenstein quoted in Mayne 1975 p.118).

To stress that the method of representation is a process of structuring which necessarily uses a structure to render the exercise comprehensible is to invite a charge of conservative formalism and/or anarchistic subjecti-vism. Brecht in his theses on Lukacs's theory of realism attempts to refute these charages by arguing that they presume an *aesthetic* sense of formalism rather than a fully social appreciation of significance: 'Every possible objection to narrative techniques such as montage, interior monologue, or the alienation effect can be raised, but it is impossible to object to them from the standpoint of realism, unless we are willing to accept a purely formalist definition of that term . . . In questions con-cerning pure forms, one must not spout nonsense in the name of Marxism; that is not Marxist, (Brecht quoted in Arvon 1973 p.107). To attempt to reduce content to a correct or proper account is to make the audience subjects, to whom things must be done so that their understanding increases; but this attempt claims as authority a timeless sense of appro-priate discourse independent of the possible realities continually being articulated: 'With the people struggling and changing reality before our eyes, we must not cling to "tried" rules of narrative, venerable literary models, eternal aesthetic laws. . . . Realistic means . . . making possible the concrete, and making possible abstraction from it' (Brecht 1974 p.50). In conclusion, therefore, we have yet another glimpse of the overlap of interests between popular art and realism. I now suggest that precisely because of its lack of self-evident authority popular art is involved in demonstrating the grounds of whatever authority is claimed. This is why the styles of authority typically claimed in a mass culture of leisure and entertainment are discussed in the next section. The search for authority is so much a feature of realist aspirations that a discussion of art knowing a world has repeatedly been led to the constitution of the world through fictional imagery: 'If we wish to have a living and combative literature, which is fully engaged with reality and fully grasps reality, a truly popular literature, we must keep step with the rapid development of reality' (*op. cit.* p.53).

Ceremonials, Play and Leisure

One reason that the relationship between popular art and realism is puzzling is that the words we use to characterize popular culture — leisure, entertainment, recreation — are all words connoting a lack of seriousness. In contrast, realism is generally understood as a word of bedrock seriousness: a recourse to realism is urged upon those who would attempt to offer political idealism — thus reality is purgative of illusion. And yet the content of performances made available by the mass media is predominantly escapist, unlikely people pursue unlikely courses of action with unlikely consequences. I have tries to clarify some features of realism but have ignored the conventional assumption that illusion is such a characteristic feature of our society. If we are to take seriously the investment of time and energy that we make in manufacturing dramas of experience that move, enthrall and excite us then surely we have to follow very closely the claim that the majority of a population are satisfied with, or indeed seek out, dramas which counterfeit the experience they attempt to express. If this is so, it is obviously of central significance for the social reality we are making. In this section I shall argue that illusions are not recognized through a disparity between them and reality, but through the forms of reality they make possible. The hobbies, entertainments and technology of contemporary leisure are undoubtedly real, the stuff of social experience, but I shall attempt to show that they constitute a museum of commodities whose only relevance is to their endless accumulation.

The predominant mode of illusion in contemporary culture has been described previously as utopianism and this term provides a convenient introduction at this point. The stories of popular culture are utopian because the ambiguity of everyday experience is suppressed in favour of a narrative structure in which the various strands of the story are resolved clearly and satisfactorily. This is not to say that there are no 'unhappy' endings, but that there is a neatness to the end of the narrative which provides a certain aesthetic satisfaction. Another aspect of utopianism which usually complements the first, although it may predominate, is stereotypical characterization, so that even if the narrative structure is more complex it may be made comprehensible by 'characters' who exemplify racial, sexual or occupational stereotypes. This process is of course intensified if the main protagonists are 'stars' who are ideal types in important respects. The utopian character of a culture of entertainment might suggest that popular narratives are legends with strong timeless features: 'My thesis . . . will be that the simplicity, the well-understood character and (connected) ritualistic quality of these two types of story is sufficient to explain their appeal both to creators and to the public . . .

These *genres* resemble nothing so much as epic poems in the style of Homer: they have heroes, trials, and ordeals. They bear some resemblance to the reality they are taken from, but are also distorted and exaggerated in the way of legends' (Jarvie 1970 p.152).

The reason why I feel dissatisfied with accounts which stress the utopian, legendary or mythic features of popular narratives is that these terms are used to imply a fundamental contrast to everyday experience. The archetypal character of such stories is stressed in order to demonstrate universal features of human 'nature' and to bring out the status of fiction as an alternative to routine reality. Tudor describes such accounts as 'aspirin analyses' in which the story seems to be 'taken' by the man in the street to relieve social pathology; the alternative does not involve denying the formulas of popular culture but treats these generalizations as attempts to: '. . . dramatize, repeat, and underline an interpretative account of acceptable social order. . . . They give the underlying regularities of our societies' concrete form' (Tudor 1974 p.218). In this context we can interpret underlying social regularities as instances of what Goffman (1976 p.69) calls 'basic social arrangements': 'They tentatively establish the terms of the contact, the mode or style of formula for the dealings that are to ensue between the persons providing the display and the persons perceiving it'. Of course the formulae of social dealings are not devices which reflect inevitable relationships, for example the dependent status of women in relation to men in our society is not inescapable, but versions of the way such relationships are to be understood: 'And what these portraits most directly tell us about is not gender, or the overall relationship between the sexes, but about *the special character and functioning of portraiture*' (*op. cit.* p.76 my emphasis). From this perspective the ceremonial character of displays or narratives is a recommendation for comprehension, it provides a form for interpretation.

It therefore seems that in order to grasp the functions of portraits we will have to pay more attention to the framing of social relationships in different types of encounter. If we use as models of fictional representation examples drawn from traditions, novel writing or theatre, then although representational conventions have distinctive properties, the finished report should be reasonably 'like' forms of action in everyday experience. In other words the devices of staging are a frame for report, they underlie representation. In other examples of fictional representation, such as children enacting a battle between legendary protagonists, representational conventions are not employed as devices to make a performance. Rather they are the performance and as such they frame constituent actions quite differently. The children are not mimicking everyday forms of action, although the imagery of enactment may be drawn from ceremonial sources like comic-strips and television series (so that death by shooting involves quite standardized clutching at heart or stomach and a peculiarly stiff way of falling), but creating illusions for an alternative to everyday reality — a reality which has to be considered on its own terms, not as a type of report. As these points have been put rather baldly I shall devote the rest of this section to a consideration of the nature of play and how it interacts with leisure.

The concept of play has existed on the edge of the human studies from their inception but has only rarely been made a central topic for discussion. In part this must be that the nature of play seems to invoke a lack of seriousness, and in part because the concept of play lacks clear boundaries and can be used to support a wide range of meanings. (There is something about this field which seems to encourage 'overviews' in which authors survey and classify some of the relevant literature; two examples which are very different to each other are Giddens 1964; Parker 1975; see also the excellent collection by Bruner 1976.) In order to demonstrate the relevance of play to my general themes I will avoid producing another survey of the field and concentrate on what has seemed to me the most salient features. The first feature of play to be emphasized is the point about a presumed lack of seriousness. In fact play is not done playfully if by that we mean casually, play is engrossing while engaged in and totally demanding. This is not to say that play is not fun or enjoyable, but that the experience of play is irreducible (Comfort 1974). The actions, the behaviour undertaken when playing have a different significance to the same actions when not playing. Therefore play is not marked off by distinct behaviour, or by a distinct attitude when participating, but by a different relationship between play and other actions which constitute the everyday world. Play lacks consequences because it encapsulates itself, we can usually choose to end the play and resume conventional responsibilities. And thus play's connotations of a lack of seriousness — it involves a suspension of conventional constraints.

Elaborating this point Omvedt (1966) introduces the idea of frame around the self that plays. Play employs a real world but uses it only 'as if' it were real, a distance is introduced between the action and its significance rather than between us and the action (there is a related use of 'as if' in relation to fictional experience in general, see for example Becker 1966). Thus to be totally absorbed in the world of play is to become a fantasist, it is to lose the sense of distance which gives us some control, a process we understand through its unconscious articulation in dreams. It is because play depends upon a sense of distance that it is necessarily metaphorical, the acting of play is a conscious exploration of analogies between a multiplicity of realities: 'Play is thus defined by a double reference, on the one hand to our normal world (the real things that are to be transformed or bracketed) and on the other to the unreality given to them' (Omvedt 1966 p.6). The metaphor has to be sustained because if it is lost the play either becomes overwhelming or too highly stylized, but a particularly powerful form of play may become a metaphor for central features of the social world. Omvedt suggests that the playful conjunction of opposites in tantric philosophy is used to simulate a sense of distance from the human context as well as the religious cosmos echoing themes of purity and pollution from the social order.

The most famous book on play is undoubtedly Huizinga (1971), and although it largely consists of a form of linguistic exploration which now seems a little archaic, there are many insights and stimulating asides (on reading Huizinga see Gombrich 1974). He begins from the premise that play is essentially the attribution of human significance. Play depends upon a sense of order that is not inherent in the actions themselves, it is therefore a way of doing that has necessarily been chosen by the participants. Significant features are ordered by human choice, we might possibly say that in this sense play is the most human of actions: as soon as it shifts from physical tumbling to explore strength and faculties, to a structured order of actions there is the crucial move from animality to humanity. The logic of this argument is that play is the essence of freedom, because if participation and manner of participation are a matter of choice they must be limited commitments, they are an acceptance of authority which can be withdrawn. (This is an encouraging contrast to most structuralist arguments where the recognition of order is welcomed as a de-humaniza-tion.) The sense of limited commitment is obviously taking up in another way the previously expressed idea that play involves a bracketing of reality, what has been less brought out so far is the dependence of play on rules (thus Wittgenstein's frequent use of the analogy between language and games). The rule-governed nature of play, through the centrality of order, might be taken to mean that play is closely linked to ritual, and although this might lead again to the speculative mists of mythic significance it does remind us of how often play is organized through games which are highly sophisticated and of literally mortal importance. It is relevant in this context to consider the example of a joker whose playing with rules to make humourous associations involves him straddling several levels of reality (see Douglas 1975).

In the points made so far I have stressed the ways in which play is articulated through a rule-based bracketing of reality, the implication of this type of formulation is that play is an activity engaged in for its own sake, there is no end result, no functional advantage to be derived from playing. There are two qualifications to this claim, the first, that play is exploratory learning, I will come back to; the second, that play in certain circumstances can express the manner of a civilization and thus define norms of elegance for that society, is an intriguing suggestion. We lack an authoritative treatment of the interpenetration of norms of elegance, as artful accomplishment, and a consciousness of civilization, as communal identity, but Huizinga speculates that one way of opening up this field would be to explore the analogies between play and style in art. Both play and style are processes of form, they provide a grammar in which specific actions are rephrased to take on an exemplary character. This may be why

attempts to discredit games through a bald description of their constituent
actions – one man hitting a piece of leather with a stick of wood – are
both quite accurate and curiously irrelevant. The kernel of the game is not
what is done but the way it is done as part of a series of actions, as with
style the formula character of that series does not prevent individual
exponents displaying their personal talents and modifications. A game is
an active depiction of a set of rules which is the text for that game, only
in certain institutional circumstances will this text be written out. A
similar distinction can be made in relation to a dramatic performance
where the 'play' is the active depiction of a text. It is in this sense that
conventional tolerance of discrepancies between composition and
performance may be taken to be an index of whether a performance is
something to be observed or made. In that in more culturally rigid
societies the composition will be more sacrosanct and the participatory
nature of the performance correspondingly devalued.

I have pointed to a link between play and style as a suggestion that
play may be functional for society in encapsulating a society's vision of
how it best does things; it provides ceremonial form for interpretation.
It is reasonable to expect that it will be easier to demonstrate such a role
in smaller, more culturally homogeneous contexts, and thus anthropo-
logical work is likely to be relevant (Geertz 1972). Geertz's paper is such
an overwhelming achievement that it is difficult to summarize; at this
stage I am concerned with his use of play as an implicit narrative. The
concept of deep play, which he takes from Bentham, refers to play where
the stakes are so high that it becomes irrational to participate, in that to
lose destroys too much. I have so far avoided competitive play but it is
obviously one type of play which necessarily threatens the bracketing of
reality, – the encouragement of success is an incipient temptation to lose
distance and control. The Balinese cockfight is such an occasion for deep
play in which the participants, although ostensibly wagering cash, are in
practice risking their status. But the risk is staged and managed in such a
way that the threat of practical consequences is generally neutralized, wins
and losses tend to balance out and thus the drama is its own rationale:
'As any art form – for that, finally, is what we are dealing with – the
cockfight renders ordinary, everyday experience comprehensible by
presenting it in terms of acts and objects which have had their practical
consequences removed and been reduced (or, if you prefer, raised) to the
level of sheer appearances, where the meaning can be more powerfully
articulated and more exactly perceived. . . . Its function is neither to
assuage social passions nor to heighten them . . . but . . . to display them'
(Geertz *op. cit.* p.23). Although each playing of the cocks is a distinct
occasion, the exemplary aura of that which is played is such that crucially
significant tones of that style of life are re-enacted: 'Quartets, still-lifes,
and cockfights are not merely reflections of a pre-existing sensibility
analogically represented; they are positive agents in the creation and

maintenance of such a sensibility' (*op. cit.* p.28).

The re-writing of functionalism in Geertz's account can introduce the other reputed functional advantage of play — that play is exploratory learning. This approach is probably most familiar through the work of Piaget and his associates and is the most commonly advanced 'explanation' of play in social-science writing. It is surprising that an 'explanation' is felt necessary, for if we examine the activity of playing it becomes evident that play is a central feature of sociality. It makes as much sense to ask to explain why humans live communally as to ask why we play; and the very inevitability of play as artful bracketing of everyday experience means that in play we necessarily explore reality: 'A third dimension of the imagination is the play system which thrives on reality problems and seeks to know the rules of how things, events, ideas, and people go together. . . . Play in this way is viewed as processing or mastering reality' (Reilly 1974 p.145; see also Foote 1954 for an unusual sense of the erotic significance of play). Thus the irreducibility of play, with which we began, does not have to be accounted for: the activity of playing is a way of organizing experience, in so doing the same world may not be constituted as in other modes of organization but the practice is not less serious. Reilly proposes that three languages exist in everyday use: dreams as visual imagery; and play as the exploration of rule-use. Through the arbitrary imposition of order the player renders the abyss (the nightmare that orderly expectations can no longer be relied upon), a source of amusement, but his very power to do so always demonstrates the precariousness of his initial understanding: 'Play is behaviour whose central mode of operations is to puzzle, to tease, to doubt at reality. The 'as-if' of the metaphor, the contradiction of the paradox, and the specificity of the rule are the realities of its substance. . . . the unknown is *homo ludens's* adventure (Reilly *op. cit.* p.141).

The implication of the remarks made so far is that play is a universal feature of human society. This does not mean, however, that we should expect to find humans playing in obviously comparable ways in all societies, the comparability will rest at the level of rule-use rather than the content of any particular set of rules. The organization of play in each society will be institutionalized in that certain 'games' will be inherited by tradition, and knowledge of their rules will be part of the taken-for-granted competence of normal members that society. Except that social conventions governing forms of play will ascribe them to different strata of society, the main criteria for distinguishing appropriate games being age, sex and social status (these are not in any order of importance). Certain forms of play are thought appropriate for children but inappropriate for adults, thus with the long progress through adulthood into old age different forms of play become more or less appropriate at different age-grades. It is equally apparent from everyday experience that play differs drastically between the sexes (again this is cross-cut by differing emphases at different age-grades), for example the rugged resistance through this century to the full admission of women as equal competitors in all events in international sporting competitions like the Olympics. Finally, access to certain forms of play has frequently been used as a mark of differing status — a familiar example is the presumed distinction in attitudes to the game between gentlemen and players in cricket.

Play as an institutionalized activity can therefore take infinite forms and be infinitely meaningful for participants and observers. Why then should it be argued that in contemporary leisure illusions are counterfeit, that they imply a reality which lacks dynamic potential? The answer to this problem lies in the differences between the words play and leisure. The former, play, refers to a mode of sociality, the latter, leisure, refers to a type of activity; to use the latter as in some sense overlapping with the former is to mistake a descriptive concept for an analytic one. Leisure is descriptive because it is a word that has acquired meanings in the context of industrial societies and is inextricably intertwined with the categorizations of property inherent in such societies. Burns (1973) points out that the growth of free time in this century is meaningful only in contrast to the century of industrialization, the pre-industrial working week, as far as it can be assessed, was probably considerably less arduous. It is in this context that the working-class struggle to restrict hours of employment as well as raise wages becomes more significant. The other facet of change consequent upon industrialization is that there has been a gradual change from direct exploitation of the work-force to an expectation of compliance through high consumption of commercial products which in turn facilitates capital mobility.

It is through both restricting hours and facilitating wide-ranging access to attractive commodities, that leisure has come to be generally understood as something that is owned rather than something that is made (cf. Birnbaum's emphasis on the fragmentation of *homo faber* in industrialization (1969)). Leisure is something that the individual or the group can keep to themselves, it is 'free' time and therefore private. The use of such a possession is demonstrated through patronage of a wide range of pursuits and activities provided by a very diffuse 'leisure industry'. The consequent circulation of resources is functional for the economy as a whole, while the very buying of individual leisure tastes encourages the feeling that the articulation of such tastes is the expression of a property right: 'The range of possible pursuits out of working time is arguably much wider than it was for any previous generation than ours. The point to be made is that these pursuits are wholly secular, organized for a commercial market, or at least for a user public, and, by and large, limited to what can be so organized' (Burns *op. cit.* p.46). The paradox is that leisure so understood necessitates becoming a member of amny audiences and yet the ultimate rationale for the pursuit of leisure is the possibility of membership. The circularity here helps to bring out that the essence of audience concern is their involement in consuming (spectating) themselves.

Leisure is therefore a type of activity which can be recognized through its dependence on commodities, the audience is entertained through the objects it chooses to possess. In the sense of conspicuous consumption this process is easily recognized, it is less easy to grasp in relation to the complementary sense of 'spending time'. Writing about urban art forms Grana (1971) cites Simmel's observation that urban life centres around a temporal paradox. Although 'urban life rhythms' are organized through conventional blocks of time for work and leisure and sleep etc., 'precisely because of that, cities are equally places where time itself becomes a luxury and where ornamental and resourceful ways of 'wasting' it provide the basis for novel, even defiant modes of social existence.' (*op. cit.* pp.70-1). Entertainment fits these terms exactly — it is ornamental, luxurious, novel and even occasionally defiant. All of these characteristics are part of it being a private expenditure of time, entertainment is above all else a conspicuous consumption of that which is both intensely personal and most quickly appropriated by holders of social power — time. It is true that the activities which provide entertainment may range from complete passivity through desultory, sporadic hobbies to long-term interests, but the problem is not that the masses are insufficiently creative in the ways they dispose of the resource of time. The problem is that leisure as a moral activity is equated with a pragmatic utilitarianism. The morality of leisure, as I have elucidated it so far, is the pursuit of those activities which most gratifyingly *fill* time. This is a waste because the imaginative participation of the audience does not sustain a distance from reality, a bracketing of the world; rather the play is immersed in the world and becomes a spectacular parody indistinguishable from any other commodity. It is in this context that leisure becomes a humanitarian problem, a responsibility for the public order.

The ideological form of contemporary leisure can be clarified by noting three features. Burns, in the previously cited paper, emphasizes the development of meanings of leisure through interaction with relevant social structure: 'The way in which people spend their disposable money and time is a mode of organizing their lives and, therefore, one of the concrete forms in which the social structure is manifest in action' (Burns *op. cit.* p.49). The fact that leisure activities are making social communities based on interest rather than neighbourhood or kinship means that such activities are an amplification of identity. The greater the autonomy the individual has in his occupational milieu the more likely there will be a blurring of the distinction between work and leisure. It is a commonplace that the second machine age is distinguished by having put an enormous control of energy facilities at the disposal of the common man, and these facilities are undoubtedly essential for the global shrinkage which is a feature of mass leisure. What is perhaps less remarked

is the use of leisure facilities to explore the edges of conventional constraints (see Mendelsohn's (1966) distinction between fantasy and reality
in his first chapter). It is in this sense that man does not make his world
through work any more but makes it through a vicarious consumption (at
its best the debate on pornography and sexuality is involved in these
issues of authentic self-exploration).

The second point is the centrality of style in the complex of allusions
and connotations which give performances an identity and links them to
a community, i.e. in this context style is being used to refer to social
projects as well as aesthetic characteristics. The importance of style grows
out of the making of lives through leisure noted in the previous paragraph:
'Leisure culture is . . . an externalized conversation of gestures, a mimetic
sphere pre-eminently concerned with the visual styling, both of the person
and the personality. From each of its related aspects we derive a strong
sense of the addiction within the culture to *form* and *style*' (Hall 1967
p.4). 'Style means the presentation of the self as a three-dimensional art
object, to be wondered at and handled' (Carter 1967 p.866). The self-
consciousness of new types of social association is therefore reinforced
and made a virtue by ransacking global exotica. Although the enormous
investment in minutiae of fashion frequently involves steam-rollering
traditional constraints, the mocking adoption of old military uniforms is
one example, the trend is in general functional for heterogeneous society.
Conflict has not disappeared from highly urbanized cultures and yet a
consistent feature of these societies has been the convergence of political
discussion towards norms of consensus. An analogous situation of a framework of assumed integration tending to mask local and sporadic, if often
very intense, conflict is generally also true of mass culture (for example the
depiction of working-class militancy in popular entertainment). The use of
style as a means of socio-cultural differentiation provides a vocabulary for
dissidence, but it frequently becomes absorbed in its own minutiae rather
than the goals it is supposed to represent.

The final point is linked to the previous two in that they seem to assume
a need to establish conventional routines, Elias and Dunning have
captured this dimension in their title 'The Quest for Excitement in
Unexciting Societies' (1967; 1969). The crux of their argument is that
complex industrial societies demand and produce a more homogeneous
and complete web of restraint than any previous social order: 'The specific
function of sport, theatre, racing, and all the other activities and events
usually associated with the term "leisure" . . . has to be assessed in relation
to this ubiquity and steadiness of excitement control. . . . In the form of
this class of leisure events our society provides for the need to experience
the upsurge of strong emotions in public — for a type of excitement which
does not disturb and endanger the relative orderliness of social life as the
serious type of excitement is likely to do' (1967 p.6). In an associated
sense Duvignaud (1972) has emphasized the significance of the event in a

world of news in which the boundaries of imagination and reality are diluted so that they imperceptibly overlap. Because the constraints of a given world can be overridden we strive to imbue every action with a theoretical dimension in which 'the instantaneous revelation of reality is more important than its description'. There has always been a spectacular dimension to popular art, a grotesque hinting at the edges of normality either through extraordinary daring or strength or through an evocation of metaphysical powers. With the advent of a mass leisure culture oriented towards continuous entertainment the spectacular has in a sense become routinized but it has also become ubiquitous so that it is pursued for its own sake. Margaret Mead makes a related point when she notes that the strength of amateur creativity has led to a routinized reproduction of conventional conceptions of artistry: 'It is not individual vision but the ability to replicate a strange commodity — individuality — which is being practised' (Mead 1960 p.20).

I have endeavoured to indicate some of the ideological force of the development of leisure as a distinct area of social experience. The structure of productive relationships in which opportunities for leisure are provided for audiences can be seen as constituting a distinctive cultural configuration, but before this can be delineated I must pay some attention to the concept of culture, 'one of the two or three most complicated words in the English language' (Williams 1976 p.76). The early uses up to around 1800 were always as 'a noun of process: the tending of something basically crops or animals' (ibid p.77). The succeeding changes in usage have, in their several forms, involved moving away from the activity of cultivation towards a more settled concept of the products of intellectual and artistic activity. This seems to me to be the core of the discussion of alienation in that such changes in use emphasize the turning away of human activity from human development to an absorption in objects as ends rather than means. In this latter sense the numerous ways of picturing, talking about and making the world become autonomous specialisms, governed by norms of appropriate practice rather than by goals of a possible human order. We can apply these features of alienation to our discussion of the differences between play and leisure. In play humans are, perhaps most characteristically, making a social order through their activities, the props of the game are the units of a code of rules but the rules themselves are irreducible. A sense of subjectivity is necessarily retained because play demands a distance from its topic, its real-ness is in its manner of being done not in the accomplished performance. Leisure, because it describes the ownership and reception of performances, is inherently centred in the commodities through which leisure is demonstrated. The subjectivity of taste is ambiguous because it bespeaks both a personal identity and the constraints of available commodities.

I have argued that play is irreducible, it either works on its own terms or it becomes absorbed into a world and it does not matter whether that world is 'real' or 'fantasy'. I have drawn some contrasts between play and leisure one of which concerns leisure's absorption in commodities, thereby making the point that leisure becomes available as performances provided by others. I wish to argue that if our analysis rests at the level of who buys what sort of leisure, then we can only offer a description of leisure as it is done. To regain a distance, so that we can get some sense of the distinctiveness of our fictions, we need to ask what sort of world is being presumed so that such and such a performance is reasonable. In previous sections I have argued that it is fruitless to search for differences between the real world and fictional depictions in terms of one version being primary, the differences rest in the type of constitutive activity we engage in when participating in real or fictional performances. Fictions presume a context which contrasts with the dramatic conventions which sustain fiction, so that we know the everyday world is 'real' because it lacks a context. The importance of talking about leisure becoming absorbed in its own commodities is that the playful fictions of contemporary leisure have lost their context. We cannot recover a context by empirical studies of what is watched because such a study presumes to 'know' the differences between observed fiction and the audience's everyday world. Instead we must focus on the sense of experience as it is formulated in popular art, precisely how the distinctiveness of fiction is recognized and sustained in a performance. This injunction demands that we do not dissolve the performance into its social background but treat seriously its own claim to distinctiveness.

If such a project is attempted we can begin to understand the ramifications of my earlier assertion that the fictions of contemporary leisure lack a context and are thus undistinguishable from any other feature of the real. The imagery of events happens in a collage of associations which transcend the distinction between real and abstract so that both only become meaningful in terms of the other. The meaning of art, as a mediation of experience in particular ideological contexts, ensures that it cannot totally transcend that context and therefore the barbarity of our age necessarily renders our art barbarous. Not just because of the administrative cruelty practised on a previously unrealized scale, but also because fetishism robs culture of one of its most important features — the sensual elaboration of experience. In a culture of entertainment hedonism is restricted to consumption and erotica necessarily become pornographic. The *promesse du bonheur* held to be intrinsic to a work of art is stunted and distorted, instead the time spent in consumption is ritualized and empty. The unity of contemporary style is not a form of life with inherent dialectical contradictions, thus it lacks the vitality of speech, instead it is a potential for use which is so universal that it precludes use; the ubiquity of form swamps all dialectical contrasts: 'Culture is a paradoxical commodity. So completely is it subject to the law of exchange that it is no longer exchanged; it is so blindly consumed in use that it can no longer be used. Therefore it amalgamates with advertising.' (Horkheimer and Adorno 1972 p.161).

The main consequence of the disorder of content ordered by style is that commercial communications become almost a living museum. Experience is ritualized in a succession of overlapping high points, a galaxy of the bizarre or otherwise noteworthy is frozen for our selection. The museum straddles our experience so that it becomes an active interpreter of that experience. As with other museums the catalogue of previous exhibits provides new criteria for the inclusion of further objects, but in this case the public are not recruited by their specialist interests but the museum is a mosaic built around the environment of a prior public. Of course the entertainment museum does not exist to enshrine the past, although there is an important necrophiliac strain, rather it enshrines the apogee of the present. However, much of that present is validated by its feeding on previous success: the future when it comes to be invented can be relied upon to be an endless reiteration of pleasures already known. The metaphor of the living museum, an environment without walls, suggests that the ubiquitous encapsulation of events has the further consequence that any scale of significance is lost. Pateman cites the phrase 'dissociated impacting' to summarize the endless but disordered flow of random information, a process that is not dysfunctional for mechanisms of social control in that it has the inherent logic of collective amnesia: 'Amnesia is a means of social control, both because it furnishes a base for undisputed triumph of official ideology, and also because by weakening the sense of personal identity it deprives people of a sense of efficacity (sic) and thus of the capacity to organize and initiate action' (Pateman 1975 p.35).

4

Narrative and Community

Medium and Message

In the course of this book I have sometimes referred to the many activities which would fall under the general heading of popular art as cultural forms, for example the cinema or the popular novel. The reason for doing this is that although there will be many different types of popular novel and individual instances will vary greatly in quality there seem to be good reasons for assuming there are distinctive features shared by all instances such that they are examples of a common form. A useful illustrative analogy here is provided by the game of football as a popular sport. Despite the wide variations in types of football match there are structural continuities between all matches and these can be summarized as a common set of rules which constitute the game to be played. In practice the cultural form of popular football consists of more than a shared set of rules, and any adequate description would have to include elements such as locally based sides with a strong communal appeal with the leading players being celebrated as stars or heroes. Similarly any discussion of popular literature as a cultural form might endeavour to identify some common rules for genre writing but would also have to include some reference to the organization of publishing, the possibilities for mass distribution and the rewards for successful authors. It is in this more general sense that in initially outlining my approach to the study of popular culture I recognized the close interdependence between the development of popular art and facilities for mass communication. Other authors have attempted to treat this interdependence more schematically and have argued that facilities for communication are effectively influential 'in their own right' — that is, that they structure how members of a society come to perceive and interpret their world. Whether or not it is possible to formulate the relationship between style of expression and means of expression as a causal one, the nature of their interdependence is intrinsically important because it deals with the organization of fictional experience both as a set of problems in social interaction and as a set of issues in the conventions of particular mode of communication.

I believe that it is possible to appreciate the significance of the relationships between style and means of expression for the organization of fictional experience from two related perspectives. First, study of the relationships between technology and meaning in public communication is another version of the relationship between form and content. In earlier chapters I have tried to show that the salience of realism as an aesthetic characterization of popular art is not accomplished in terms of manifest fidelity to an agreed 'external' world, but is demonstrated through the aesthetic imagery being accepted as a way of portraying that world. In the case of realism I therefore attempted to replace a conventional distinction between form and content by pointing to the ways in which form, as the premises for imaginative participation, provides for the significance of shifting aspects of imagery and articulation. In this chapter I shall attempt to show that a consistent approach can be adopted in relation to the study of changes in means of expression. The second perspective concerns the implications of trying to provide a history of communication. I have argued that art history, because its practitioners work within the constraints of an extrapolation from text to author, provides a schematization of artistic significance which is ideological through presuming a level of independent aesthetic import. If a history of communicative practices were similar in that the author tried to derive social effects from communicative causes, i.e. attempted to assess the implications of innovations in technology for communication, then it could be argued that he was engaging in a related process of ideological mystification. I hope to argue that the implications of changing communication facilities do not derive simply from the technology, but from a complex process of refraction through the communal social structure in which those facilities are articulated.

In order to clarify some of these points I shall discuss the relationship between communicative forms and narrative structure. I shall begin with some aspects of shifts in visual literacy. I keep to the slightly more clumsy visual rather than pictorial representation here because I want the framework of the discussion to be able to include material such as masks, prints and video-films etc., as well as more conventionally understood 'pictures'. The concept of visual literacy may seem at first a puzzling idea. Our ability to see and to know what we see, except of course for those with some degree of visual handicap, is an attribute we take for granted; and at first sight there would seem to be no intrinsic reason why members of different cultures should experience their visual environment differently. The flaw with these truisms is that they rest on a mental image of natural man responding to an environment that is also natural — unstructured by other humans. In practice these conditions do not hold, we live in a world which is saturated with human intention visible through semiotic imagery which denotes and connotes complexities of meaning to those competent to negotiate the environment. The cultural resources of ordinary membership can therefore be expected to include a grasp of local

conventions of visual 'legibility'. Visual literacy is therefore to be understood as the study of communication through the sense of sight: 'Visual
literacy implies understanding, the means of seeing and sharing meaning
with some level of predictable universality. To accomplish this requires
reaching beyond the innate visual powers of the human organism'
(Dondis 1973 p.182). Dondis continues to explain what he means by
'going beyond innate powers' by the analogy of the verbally literate person
who can use knowledge of a language to develop others' understanding. To
be visually literate is to be able to manipulate representational conventions
to express new ideas — and implicitly therefore to be able to change conventions to take advantage of new facilities.

The most salient connotation of a concept of literacy is that conventions of perception constitute a language and that this language might in
certain circumstances be recorded such that it could be taught or learnt.
Goody and Watt (1968 p.27) have suggested that language marks one
boundary between human studies, in that popular literacy distinguishes
between the domains of anthropologist and sociologist, and therefore in
relation to popular fiction we ought to be particularly sensitive to the
social transmission of vernacular symbolism. The essence of symbolism is
the ability to associate ideas, to devise labels which can be used independently of the presence of that which was the original subject of the label.
Thus the ability to symbolize means that imagery is not just reflexive but
can be used persuasively, mateaphorically, to imagine possibilities and
recollections. It is in this sense that one can say that the ability to con-
verse enables man to straddle time, he is no longer confined to the present.
The ability to devise a visual representation is closely related in that the
image straddles space rather than time. Space is by definition the invisible
boundary of physical form, it becomes structured when man begins to
attempt architecturally to enclose it. To abstract elements from the
physical environment as subjects for representation is to fracture their
spatial setting and impose a persuasive alternative. The use of representational resources in the least complex social orders can be divided into two
distinct forms. The first is constructing more stable dwellings in which the
physical order can more precisely express the social order. The second is
to render images and depictions of objects and animals significant to the
community. The two forms will interrelate and a more complex 'language'
of imagery and structure will characterize different cultures (for an
unusual collection of papers exploring these interrelationships see Oliver
1975). But at first before there is a vocabulary of architectural form
visual representation will be raw and unmediated.

To expand this argument a little, one can say that as pre-historical
visual representation lacks a humanly structured environment its authors
have to utilize features of the natural environment. So that features of
the contours of a cave wall, or a stick or tusk are moulded to provide the
basis of visual representation. In this sense one can say that primitive visual

literacy is unframed, the images and forms are 'drawn out' of a given physical environment and lack a syntax to structure each image or the jumble of imagery (Schapiro, 1969, includes some interesting discussion of the implications of frames for pictorial representation). A rather bastardized contemporary version of visual literacy might be the graffitti sprayed on public facilities. Giedion (1960) has argued that the lack of concepts of architectural space meant that primeval artists could not prescribe a particular standpoint from which their work should be read. Therefore the images are syntactically incoherent in terms of our criteria of legibility, their authors worked with inadequate, flickering light and their images flicker into our focus. The argument is enhanced by noting two further features of prehistoric cave paintings, the first is that through time successive artists overlaid new images on the work of their predecessors — although they were usually careful to avoid unnecessary damage. The second is that the images were private and secret, difficult to get at and often drawn on walls and ceilings not normally visible to a visitor.

It seems reasonable to argue then that such art was undertaken for a different purpose from our conventional expectations, the images were perhaps a naming of significant features of the environment as a more or less religious evocation. The representations are not illiterate because they are not designed to be read as a record, they are images which solely celebrate themselves. Visual literacy could only become syntactically coherent through the development of concepts of architectural space. I am therefore arguing that the language of perception is the social organization of space. Imagery whether it is a pattern on a domestic implement, or the shape of a receptacle used at a religious ceremony, or the stylized representation of an animal, a god or a clan (and perhaps all three simultaneously), is the plastic imposition of form on incoherent substance. By social organization of space I do not necessarily mean an enclosure of space, as in a house, but an ability to see shape (form) as the medium of human fabrication. Vernacular symbolism can be seen to depend upon the development of a humanly structured environment in which the resources of space, colour, structure etc., as well as locally available material, were part of the cultural vocabulary of the community.

This argument might be interpreted to mean that the control of space through human composition was to visual communication what the development of a means of recording a language graphically was to oral communication. I do not believe this to be the case, and in showing the difference between implications of changing forms of expression I hope to bring out a more general argument about the relationship between technology and consciousness. Without reviewing the literature in detail I can briefly summarize the implication of verbal literacy as 'the fact that writing establishes a different kind of relationship between the word and its referent, a relationship that is more general and more abstract, and less closely connected with the particularities of person, place and time, than obtains in oral communication' (Goody and Watt 1968 p.44). The move to abstraction opened up the intellectual self-consciousness of political communities in two ways. The first is that the boundaries of the community as a cognitive and economic enclave can be crossed. Of course members of a preliterate society may be aware of the existence of and trade with neighbouring societies, but the acquisition of literacy, both communally and psychologically, provides a framework for comparative exchange and a basis for explanatory inquiry — traditional rationality can be challenged (for some interestingly relevant discussion see Fuglesang 1973). The second aspect of the move to abstraction can be summarized as the development of a possible distinction between myth and history — that is that we can aspire to know the world as it is rather than as the vehicle for our community.

If we compare this discussion to the relationship between visual communication and architectural space it seems inappropriate to suggest that the ability to manipulate devices of space, colour and structure etc., provided for intellectual scepticism in the sense of the previous paragraph. These devices are the phonemes of visual communication, the patterns of their association in a particular culture make it distinctive and idiosyncratic. To extend the metaphor one can say that visual phonemes do not become concretized in the sense that they become self-conscious, abstractable from their community of use, until they become either a commodity or reproducible. When a style of imagery can be valued and prized as a cultural form which has a distinctive significance for the community, then the examples or instances of that style are 'statements' which relate to a tradition or ceremonial language. This tradition may serve important ritual functions in the community, celebrating the collective art of imposing order (see in particular Fernandez 1974, but there are several other relevant papers in the collection edited by d'Azevedo), but more immediately relevant for this discussion is that it is institutionalized. The tradition exists as something that can be taught or learnt, so that although some skill in the craft may be a common cultural resource, particularly gifted specialists will be praised as admired masters. Specialists in traditional imagery, who can quite legitimately be called artists, seem to occupy somewhat ambiguous status ranking. They may be admired for their individual skill but their collective craft, whether or not its practitioners constitute a distinct caste, is often held to be a low-status occupation whose practitioners are unreliable and incompetent outside the practice of their craft skills (in addition to the collection cited above see also Forge 1973). The existence of a tradition with its associated social practices of production, distribution and criticism constitutes a cultural form with a distinctive relationship between representational conventions and the community in which these conventions are appreciated and employed. The cultural form is distinctive through its potential for expressing collective experience for the community.

In suggesting that traditions of aesthetic expression can be understood as ceremonial languages I am not arguing there is a direct parallel between the emancipatory power of literacy and the cultural functions of tradition. A form of communication only has meaningful implications for interpretive styles in a community if the intellectual potential is socially articulated. The point may be illustrated by a later paper by Jack Goody (1968) in which, in introducing the original paper by himself and Watt on literacy, he considers some of the reasons why critics of that paper had argued that it had exaggerated the consequences of literacy. In order to understand why the potential of literacy had been unevenly exploited Goody argues that we have to undertake the ethnography of written communication in different societies. Amongst the reasons he cites are situations in which there is a close identification between writing and religious knowledge. Here the technique is socially understood as an aid to the significance of content and is therefore subordinate to orthodoxy: 'What was formerly oral now gets set down in writing and just as religious myths become crystallized in the words of the Holy Book, so too magical formulae become perpetuated in the spae-books, grimoires and numerological treatises that spread throughout the literate world.' (*op. cit.* p.16). There may therefore be a situation of cultural lag in which the facilities of writing are not fully explored but are used as an adjunct to traditional structures of thought and education. Essentially the core of restraint upon communicative facility whether it was in terms of religious tradition as in India, or through the restrictions of the non-alphabetic script as in China was to underlie an intellectual culture of antiquarianism and literary exclusiveness which 'enabled knowledge to be confined to a small percentage of people' (*op. cit.* p.24). The languages of expression in a community, whether they are traditional cultural forms or means of inscribing speech, are facilities whose use is structured by the understanding of community endorsed by those groups who exercise power in that community.

My argument is therefore that we cannot hope to plug in the development of a new communicative facility as a sufficient explanation of shifts in the cognitive order of a culture. Taking the example of visual literacy we can see that the development of the syntactical conventions we conveniently refer to as West European perspective is a central feature of the history of our visual sensibility. We would be surprised if it were suggested that the development of pictorial perspective was completely coincidental with other changes in European humanism, features such as the secularization of political philosophy and the emergence of personal rather than epic narratives. But the interconnectedness of these changes in intellectual structure and preconceptions was an articulation of social possibility not a precondition of social change — although communicative forms undoubtedly have cumulative implications for social change (see for example Eisenstein's (1969) stimulating discussion of the significance of printing for the Renaissance; an approach she later summarizes as: 'I believe we can enlarge, rather than narrow, our understanding of the new ethos by relating it to a change in communicative systems' (1971 p.141)). The history of visual literacy is by nature of its subject matter more diffuse than the history of languages. This is because shifts in style and expressive form are usually moves in terms of shading, emphasis, perhaps even vitality, rather than a marked jump in structuring conventions. Structural continuity does not mean, however, that variations in expressive style must be seen as personal idiosyncrasies, it is possibly because visual literacy is so intermeshed with all other uses of tangible form in a culture that the conventions of visual form are so sensitive to social expectations and functions (an interesting discussion occasionally relevant to this argument and outside the usual confines of post-Renaissance history is Pollitt 1972). The artists in tribal society are not reduced to automatons because they are working through what are usually highly organized categories for expression. Innovation in such a context cannot be fostered by 'training' an artist or by arbitrarily introducing a new framework for facilities for the work; for example tribal art which has become a resource for tourists to collect may echo the external formulae of previous work in the tradition but do so in a mechanical, closed manner (cf. Laude 1971). The conventions of visual representation are necessarily mediated through communicative facilities so that meaningful expression is complexly embedded, but in the dialectic of aesthetic force the meaning comes from the *use* of conventions and facilities not from some sense of inherent logic.

I have suggested that visual literacy is so embedded or intermeshed with all other uses of tangible form in a culture that representational conventions are peculiarly inseparable from other aspects of cultural style. If this suggestion is correct we should expect visual literacy to be a 'conservative' cultural idiom, a shared characteristic that is resistant to pressures to change. But in the course of the last century a series of technological innovations has made possible exact replicas of features of the world and other modes of representation. These innovations can be summarized as the facility to produce faithful representations of subjects so that these subjects themselves could be faithfully reproduced. Obviously such innovations are likely to transform the significance of representations in all the sciences as well as in fictional reports, both because the phenomenal features of the subject can be recorded exactly and when a distinctive perspective on the subject is relevant that distinctive perspective can be reproduced. This combination of points is slightly confusing: the idea here is that the image obtained by inserting a camera into a human body is a record of what anyone would find there and also that the image can be exactly reproduced an infinite number of times (and therefore that the 'subjective' representations such as botanical drawings can have their distinctiveness reproduced.) These facilities are possible because we have 'at last achieved a way of making visual reports that had no interfering symbolic linear syntax of their own' (Ivins 1953 p.177). I do not think it necessary to examine in any detail the extent to which this proposition is literally true. Ivins himself makes several qualifications of his own claim such as the properties of lens, the mobility of the camera and the photographic emphasis upon the particular rather than the general. The implications of technological change for graphic arts have in any case been more exhaustively explored by Jussim (1974). What is relevant here is that technological facilities were understood at the time of their development to be transcending the limitations of personal vision.

It is because the facilities of photographic technology could be seen to be placing tools in the hands of the collectivity rather than enhancing the acquisitions of individuals that they were so intimately caught up with other processes in the development of popular culture. I have noted before that there is a close relationship between ethnography, as the record of communal life, and popular art, as the representation of communal experience. Photographic technology offers an impersonal record of the collectivity which exactly straddles the difference between life as everyday habits and experience as a selection of significant features. The technology was therefore able to be used to exploit precisely the features encouraged by fictional ethnography, that is that such ethnographies will be acquisitive, spectacular and authoritative. Photography is essentially acquisitive: whether it is a record of family events such as the biography of children and unique celebrations — golden weddings etc., — or reports from exotic places, again either true voyages of exploration or part of the paraphernalia of tourism, the photograph can be used to freeze that moment of experience and package it so that it can be reproduced and recollected for an appropriate audience. Photographic equipment is the archetypal means of staging spectacular reports. Fictional ethnographies are likely to seek to transcend the mundane in favour of exotica or the breathtaking. Visual gadgetry in the nineteenth century usually went through two stages of, at first, being a domestic plaything even if some of the effects aspired to the spectacular (cf. Klingender 1972 esp. p.86), to facilitating dramatic force and verisimilitude in public performance. Finally, fictional ethnography will aspire to present its narrative stance as authoritative, as a report that would be agreed to by all reasonable members of the collectivity. In relation to photography the narrative stance of the camera is authoritative through several distinctive features: '1 by option we see not normally but differently; 2 in some measure we can control where and how we do see beyond the normal limitations; 3 our relation to the objects of our scrutiny assumes a kind of "closeness" which is unique to the contrived perception and which disappears when that experience ceases' (Fell 1974 p.123).

The concept of narrative stance is important because it brings out some features of changes in popular art which I have attempted to describe and elucidate before. The technology of visual display can be summarized as providing a public privacy. The super-human visionary powers of the medium of display meant that each individual was privileged to transcend the literal distance between himself and the subject of the performance. The implication of treating the means of report as the eye of the audience is that 'the viewer is encouraged to assume a point of view that is both unique and judgemental to the story, he . . . has become "involved". The election of "angle" is a matter of consequence' (Fell *op. cit.* p.181). In one sense therefore the performances available through the facilities of the developing technology were more likely to be gripping through identification — participation is a necessary consequence of attention. And yet because the participation was vicarious, it physically enacted the medium of presentation, Brecht's audience member was cast into a situation of passivity: 'The theatre as we know shows the structure of society (represented on the stage) as incapable of being influenced by society (in the auditorium)' (Brecht in Willett 1964 p.189). As Fell argues, the narrative complexity of filmic vision means that it can be seen as a poor man's version of cubism, that the coalescence of diverse elements from a jumble of spatial and temporal contexts in the simultaneous present of the flickering screen is a popular articulation of the relativities of twentieth-century consciousness. And yet the crucial distinction between lived experience and fictional experience is not superseded, the structure of the story is still dependent upon genre formulae and as such is produced principally as a medium of commercial exchange.

I believe it is possible to appreciate the close interdependence between the developing cultural forms of popular art and technical innovations such as those associated with photography through a study of a prominent narrative formula. I have chosen the example of melodrama because of its persistent popularity and because the 'classic' structure of melodrama can be argued to be a template for the heterogeneous narratives of popular fiction. Cawelti (1976 p.264) describes the structure of melodrama as a combination of a detailed, often critical picture of a social setting through which multiple strands of plot and character are pulled, overlaid with a version of the moral order in which conventional verities are reaffirmed; 'The greater gloom and uncertainty the melodramatist can plunge us into, before revealing the basic morality and order of the world, the more fully he can achieve the basic effect of melodrama'. The heightened interest the author attempts to produce in us is maintained by recurrent crises with often spectacular implications. The narrative force of melodrama therefore derives from piling incidents one upon the other, either through a grotesque succession of adventures for a limited cast or through involving a wide range of social types (with appropriate histories), in a more specific social setting. It might seem that the combination of multiple narrative incidents with a common concern with sexual dangers (and particularly in con-temporary melodramas cloying portraits of sexual relationships), justifies characterizing the frisson of melodrama as respectable pornography. I think this would be mistaken because pornography is concerned with sexual relationships to the exclusion of all else, melodrama uses sexual tension to justify reasserting the values of 'social dominance, the ideas of middle-class domesticity, the dream of romantic love, and the drive for social mobility.' (*op. cit.* p.269; Cawelti's summary actually refers to the earliest melodramas but, as he recognizes, these values have persisted.).

The narrative formula of melodrama was developed by photographic technology in a number of ways. First was the necessary relationship between melodrama and situational development, the 'stage' had literally to be set — for largely unsophisticated audiences — through the depiction of characters and setting in such a way that the unfolding of events was explicable and reasonably engrossing. A second reason is that the sub-species of melodramatic imagination, for example historical spectacular, romantic adventure, urban crime and gothic horror, could not only be adapted to the new mode of performance but were also extremely functional for industries making large numbers of cheap dramas both for large audiences and to cater to established 'category tastes'. There were therefore continuities between the established codes of urban entertinment and the developing technology of nascent mass entertainment. In part this was explicable by human continuities, the same motley collection of entertainers, showmen and con men who populated the fringes of Victorian cautionary literature were the first to grasp the commercial potential of the new facilities (Briggs 1960; see also the backgrounds of the subjects in French 1971). And in part because it was the social organization of fictional experience in all media of popular art that was changing, not just a response to new technological facilities: '. . . sub-literature shares several elements with early movies: a guaranteed audience, simplistic stories and characterizations, middle-class morality genres, the costumes of melodrama, and plots like exoskeletons. What appears most striking is that amid all this trivia there developed a particular kind of mimed action-description that impressively anticipates the strengths of analogous movie forms' (Fell *op. cit.* p.38).

My argument is that if we consider the instances of possible changes in visual literacy in popular experience related to technological innovation, we can begin to grasp how expectations were articulated through narrative form. The starting-point for such an analysis must be the accessibility of mass audiences to commercial exploitation, or conversely their demands for play and entertainment in a barren urban environment. The two, accessibility and demand, are not of course equivalent — there is a logic to commercialism which promotes centralization and standardization and the mass audience has by and large acquiesced to this pressure; but it was not an inevitable process as the demand could have been satisfied through more locally heterogeneous and communally self-conscious forms of entertainment. Partly through the paucity of skilled producers, and partly because of the naivety of audiences, and partly through capitalist stimulation of demand the voracious appetite for urban entertainment was satisfied in general through ringing the changes on certain narrative formulae. The interdependence of these moments in social taste — on the one hand audience massification and on the other narrative formulaization — is articulated and displayed through conventions of expressive style, a narrative form, which I can perhaps best characterize through the phrase coherent surrealism: coherent in that the imaginative tracery with which the story is embellished has to be consistent with the underlying formula and correspond to the logic of characterization, for example national, racial or sexual stereotypes; realistic through the use of public details in signposting the story's development rather than through depth of characterization; and surrealistic because the imagery gave a vicarious omniscience to the audience and the styles could celebrate this garish multiplicity of perspectives (this is perhaps one of the reasons why self-conscious modernists like constructivists and surrealists have often acknowledged their debts to popular art). These facets of popular narrative form stimulated and were stimulated by the facilities of photographic technology, but the visual literacy they utilized was a mode of cognition, a way of shaping experience to expectations, not a product of technological imperatives.

I have tried to avoid becoming ensnared in the complexities of particular versions of communicative determinism because I think it more important to elucidate the general relationships between narrative forms and constitutive social expectations. However, the work of perhaps the most well known exponent of emphasising the medium rather than the message, Marshall McLuhan, is worth noting in a couple of respects that relate to my main concerns. The first is that the ideology of technological determinism is only possible if the theorist has first mistaken the nature of the relationship between language and expression. The idea that language structures thought can be meant in either a weak sense of recognizing that different groups have special interests which are expressed in more complex lexical differentiation — thus the famous case of Eskimo discrimination between types of snow. There is another stronger sense in which it is argued that the grammatical structure of a particular language articulates (and conversely restricts) certain cognitive possibilities (Whorf's central examples were taken from the language of the Hopi tribe in North America, the relevant literature is fully discussed in Penn (1972) and Rossi-Landi (1973), the most direct link to McLuhan is through the work of Dorothy Lee (1959)). It is commonplace to point to the logical, as well as substantive, difficulties with this strong version of linguistic relativism: the most obvious is the paradox involved in denying the possibility of translation through the use of instances which can only begin to be relevant through some grasp of what translation should be like. Theorists of linguistic determinism become involved in these problems because of a conceptual distinction between a language, as a means of expression, and that which is to be expressed. It is assumed that there are mechanisms of interaction, such as senses, language or technologies, which exist to be used. The alternative perspective developed here is that language (as a general name for processes of interaction) only exists as it is practiced to say 'something', and the 'thing' said is in part the form of the expression used.

All forms of determinism (whether technical or historical) essentially derogate human authority by rendering it subject to non-human mystifying constraints. In McLuhan's (1964) case the process is more ambiguous because the intention is ostensibly to celebrate our regaining faculties which had been arbitrarily restricted by print technologies, but in fact the 'celebration' has distinct ideological implications. These can be introduced by a successful analogy Jonathan Miller (1971 p.100) draws in discussing an alternative to McLuhan: 'Language in fact bears the same relationship to the concept of mind that legislation bears to the concept of parliament: it is a competence forever bodying itself in a series of concrete performances' (for another interesting discussion of McLuhan's work see Fekete 1973). Both communication and legislation are political because they are an articulation of intentions, prejudices and expectations etc., and are primarily significant through the polical judgements they display. Thus to celebrate the use of modernist iconography in advertising imagery without noting the commercial values which advertising predicates is to abstract the means from its political context. At this level the temporary commercial success of McLuhan is presumably just an index of the degree of delighted surprise amongst conventionally derided groups, like advertising and public relations men, at finding an academic who seemed to find virtue in their work. More seriously, the political naivety of a communications focus occasionally leads to absurdities such as: 'Is it not strange that the Marxists should have no awareness of the means of communication as the constitutive social factor? That Marx should not have noticed that English and American industry were merely projections of print technology?' (McLuhan 1967, No. 2). Such sentiments are obviously likely to appeal to proponents of social engineering who would search for technocratic solutions to social problems and who would advocate a science of society independent of the social order of 'knowledge' production. McLuhan is not in fact a social engineer but attempts an extraordinary reconciliation of Roman Catholic universalism with the 'literacy' of contemporary popular art. In this he is providing another perspective on the relationships between the civilized community and the mass public of urban popular art that is the recurrent theme of cultural criticism in industrial societies.

McLuhan was for some years reported as a cultural prophet in the media, in part because his ideas were taken up within the counter-culture. This version of McLuhanism is interesting because it pushes the metaphor of literacy to its extreme. If means of communication are modes of consciousness because they structure what can be known and thereby promote characteristic ways of thinking, then (a) grasp of technology for communication becomes in itself an extension of literacy; and (b) an extension of means of communication can be seen as an extension, expansion, of consciousness. These theses are given a further gloss by adapting some terminology from computer use so that structures of association within sign systems can be seen as analytic logics which provide a further transformation of consciousness. I do not deny that there are contemporary developments in technology which do constitute a significant extension of communicative facilities, but consistent with my other arguments I believe that the implications of these facilities mainly derives from the relations of production through which they are produced and distributed. The institutionalization of facilities for expression through which a cultural form takes on characteristic features such as genres, types of star and narrative stance, cannot be separated from other institutional structures in that society. In Erik Barnouw's (1975 p.60) excellent history of American broadcasting he brings out clearly the implications of conceiving broadcasting facilities as channels of transmission in which the broadcaster was a 'neutral' distributor: 'The industry had now arrived at a structure that would hold for years: a nationwide system based on advertising; a network linked by cables of the telephone system; stations on temporary licenses; a regulatory commission.' (Williams, 1974, interestingly discusses the institutionalization of television with particular reference to Britain; see also Wilson's (1961) study of the pressures which led to the introduction of commercial television in Britain.) The cultural form which embodies the facilities of a medium is in practice the working out of a series of presuppositions about relationships within the collectivity.

It is because the responses of critics to the massification of art is a necessary part of the cultural history of these implications of massification that McLuhan is relevant to this essay. McLuhan's conservatism is consistent with more 'pessimistic' responses to massification (despite the 'optimism' of his discovery of post-literate man) both because he depoliticizes social change; but more importantly because he colludes in a concept of community as a form of consciousness. In the present context I can use a distinction between public and audience as a way of clarifying a distinction between types of cultural community. In a classic conservative response to the development of authorship for a mass reading public (I am leaving on one side for the present the empirical adequacy of the account) Q.D. Leavis (1965) was centrally concerned with the disintegration of the reading public under commercial pressures. This public, a community of like-minded readers, became an audience, a fragmented, heterogeneous receptacle for undiscriminating uniformity. That is, if the community is conceptualized as a shared form of consciousness it becomes possible to divide people into a public, those who can participate,

and an audience, those empty vessels who merely respond. McLuhan's
conceptual framework does not contradict these distinctions, he differs
in that he argues that the public was characteristically restricted and that
the audience has new opportunities for innovative communalization; but
he retains the crucial assumption that cultural mediation is a process
of mental empathy. Thus the conservative response to the development
of mass culture always consists of a number of interpretive problems
turning around the empathetic possibilities in popular art. The alternative
approach understands popular art as opportunities for constituting
fictional experience and therefore distinguishes between public and
audience as points on a scale of greater or lesser opportunity to participate
in available cultural forms. An approach which makes the practice of
authorship considerably more responsible, and thereby raises problems I
consider in the next section.

Authorship

A recurrent image in social theory is to represent the relationship
between culture and community as analogous to the relationship of brain
and hands. At the level of the collectivity, culture comprises the intellectual and emotional perceptions of individuals while the community
comprizes tangible actions which shape and coerce material resources. Of
course the distinction is untenable in any rigorous way but the image has
a representational power in that it directs attention to the reformulation
of 'reality' in social practice. Our attention is so directed because the
distinction tacitly accepts that the world of material resources is structured and made finite by the cultural resources available to the members
of a collectivity. We therefore accept that the social reality we share with
our neighbours is not something given to us finished and complete before
our birth but is adapted, developed and in an important sense made by us
in the course of living that reality. If we say that the real is effectively
delimited by our powers of perception and comprehension, then this will
have interesting consequences for any attempt to define fictional or symbolic representations. To accept as a starting-point that social thought is
not a mirror-like response to 'the facts of the case', then all types of
representation are more or less artful. This raises a series of questions
about how the members of a collectivity order a continuum of artfulness.
A possible answer is in terms of established forms for different types of
representational work, for example the differences between a novel and
an experimental report. This directs our attention to how genres develop,
become institutionalized and then gradually lose evocative force. Although
these problems of social judgement will be occasionally puzzling for
individuals, as in the example of someone seeing a television play as a
literal report, usually the resources of competent membership will be
sufficient to enable them to respond appropriately. I suggest that these

resources shared by virtue by being members of something held in common in effect constitute a culture, so that a culture is to be understood as resources for representational work which are held in common. The initial advantage is that it directs attention to differences between types or forms of representational work, rather than the content of any particular narrative. A related advantage is that the sphere of cultural analysis is firmly situated at the level of resources held in common, i.e. collective styles or characteristic manners, and not at the level of the individual so that idiosyncratic narrative skills are not over-emphasized.

The 'other side' of this formulation is that the social negotiation of differences between modes of representational work provides an opportunity to elucidate cultural experience. In the same way and for the same reasons that one would not want to say that the ability to participate in a verbal encounter was dependent upon a competent grasp of rules of grammatical structure, (to elaborate this rather bald assertion see Goffman 1976), so the ability to participate in a fictional performance involves more than a (possibly unconscious) sense of rules for story-telling. I mean participate in the loosest sense of being involved at any stage either with production or as a member of an audience (and in this sense the opportunities for participation for an audience member is a relationship of production in the same way as being employed in a production organization). To illustrate what I mean we can use the example of the commercial cinema. There is by now what seems an enormous literature on the semiotics of film in which the analyst seeks to uncover the devices through which the narrative is unfolded. However loosely one speaks, presumably a competent member of an audience attends to at least some of these devices in following the narrative, and thus such devices relate to that member's ability. But in the same way that speaking is more than being grammatical, participation in an audience involves more than abstract cognitive skills. We can distinguish two levels of performative participation (negotiation), the first is those social skills displayed in buying tickets, finding one's seat, observing the conventions of attention and applause and managing exiting. The second level is only analytically distinguishable from the first, but it relates to the development of identity involved in attending performances of a distinct style. For the sake of convenience I will continue to speak of individual identity but the analysis is equally relevant to the development of collective taste. By patronizing a certain type of performance an individual is asserting a conception of self with distinctive aesthetic tastes and communal affiliations. This may be difficult to accept in relation to one occasion but through time the majority of people acquire consistent tastes which are responded to by significant others so that identity is accumulated.

To return to my opening image, I now want to suggest that culture is not a corpus of mental entities, processes or resources which, like ghosts in a machine, inhabit a more tangibly available social world, but is better understood as the opportunities for constitutive participation in modes of representation. It is through these opportunities that a shared social reality is practically accomplished. Briefly elaborating each of these concepts: by opportunities I mean my recurrent concern with relations of production, so that shifts in the social organization of cultural production will have implications for the sort of cultural work accomplished; by constitutive participation I mean the concept of social negotiation discussed in the previous paragraph, the organization of narrative relationships through which the performance is accomplished (the most relevant illustration in this essay comes in the discussion of the shift from play to leisure); by modes of representation I mean the instituionalized forms and styles of expression available in a particular society, not only forms such as easel-painting and the novel — I intended the discussion of public experience in the final part of the second chapter to illustrate a 'language' of representation and the sort of cultural meanings it was peculiarly appropriate to convey. This formulation of cultural experience is opposed to the ideological implications of understanding as empathetic appreciation, I suggest instead that appreciation is participation in the process through which opportunities for production become translated into performance.

I believe that this suggestion is considerably more appropriate when we are concerned with the implications of different contexts of appreciation. If, for example, we wished to contrast reggae as it is performed and experienced in Jamaica with its appreciation as an imported music in Britain and North America we could not base our analyses on the performances alone, even if we included some obligatory reference to context. In Jamaica the music is embedded in the community, so that bands are unstable amalgamations and performances, both concerts and recordings, have strong impromptu features, so the music expresses the bitterness of unemployed male youths. Of course, it may be significant that both the strong communal ties and the bitterness are metaphorically associated with what the audience overseas sees the music articulating for them, but the associations are metaphorical now because the social organization of cultural experience has changed. I emphasize that the approach I am trying to develop here is centrally characterized by a concern with how culture is accomplished. This is an important change from the bulk of material on cultural issues which when it gets beyond a critical concern with 'what' questions (what does this performance mean?), is usually phrased in terms of 'why' questions (why was it done in such a way?). My dissatisfaction with questions about 'why' is that their logic suggests answers are to be found through investigating authors — or if they are more social, of authors as voices of a class ideology. I believe this approach to be inappropriate because, particularly in the area of popular art, authors' motives are empirically untraceable. More seriously, I do not believe that motives, or cultural indicators, are things which exist in themselves but they are interpretive devices which enable us to 'make sense' of performances. I believe it to be the proper business of sociology to inquire into the possible sense — for different groups in different socio-historical circumstances — which can be made.

The distinction I wish to identify is one between the ostensible subject matter of a performance, which in the case of popular art is very often a highly routinized story, and the type of enactment which the performance facilitates. I hope I can find a clarifying illustration in the class of popular entertainments which covers street games, revels, traditional festivals and sporting encounters. These entertainments are popular art, and their history illustrates many of the points made in this book concerning the routinization of spectacle (for example contemporary professional football), but their significance cannot be said to consist of what is ostensibly going on. Even when spectators are attracted by particularly skillful performers their response is only partly aesthetic appreciation, considerable enthusiasm is generated by the players serving as an emblem for, an enactment of, the collectivity. I therefore wish to argue that there is a level of significance to performance which can only be understood by attempting to elucidate what sort of collectivity is being pointed to in performance. It is not ironic but inherent in the approach being developed that our grasp of this argument is probably best developed through works of art which have tried to express for themselves the constitutive significance of fictional experience (although he uses a different theoretical vocabulary I have found Richard Hoggart's book (1957) an important inspiration for this argument).

I wish to argue that analysis of the significance of popular art in contemporary society will have to work with a broad conception of facilities for making performances. In a very preliminary way one can suggest three levels of facilities, levels which although they are increasingly abstract relate very importantly to understanding cultural change. The first level of facility can be headed patronage and staging and is essentially concerned with the organization of financial support for producers while they are developing a performance and the organization of capital resources so that the performance can be staged and distributed. The role of the Arts Council in providing bursaries for authors and supporting a book club for the distribution of new novels fits fairly easily into this heading, but I believe it does not strain the terms too much to interpret the employment situation at a large organization such as a television company as providing another version of the same sort of relationship. The second level of facility I shall call styles, and refers to those differences in ways of story-telling types of enactment, that I have previously described as modes of representation. These idioms of expression are resources in that although individual authors may adopt and develop them, they are ways of working which cannot really be traced to individuals and whose terms structure the story told — it is in this way that one can see the validity of describing

these styles as 'languages'. The third level of facility is the most difficult
to describe concisely but it takes up the idea that if an individual, or a
group, is to represent social experience as fictive experience then the
author has to find some way of situating himself *vis-à-vis* the social such
that he can more or less self-consciously refashion 'it'; inherent in that
point is the implication that he must be accepted by significant others as
carrying-off that 'situating'. It is because this process is only seen as
difficult in circumstances of cultural transition that we can see that it is
conventionally accomplished through the use of cultural facilities, and
that the nature of these facilities will change in relation to other changes
in the collectivity.

One can illustrate this thesis by pointing to examples of differences
in responsibility for authorship amongst the general type which might be
described as authors for new proletarian readership. The backcloth for
the discussion of popular art throughout the essay has been the development of huge conglomerations of wage labourers in urban centres and
the exploitation of communicative resources in entertaining and stimulating and politicizing these anonymous masses. Although the bulk of
popular art produced in this context will be highly stylized and produced
anonymously, there will be a body of work in which the social position
of the audience will be an important factor in informing the narrative
structure of the work. To be more specific one can say that amongst the
literature produced for the mass reading public there will be a number of
books in which the authors do not take the social structure for granted
but use it as a factor which informs and shapes narrative development.
This might be most familiar to us through the romantic genre in which the
principal protagonists are kept apart by the structural barriers of unequal
social status, but there is also a considerable amount of work in which
the political implications of structural inequalities are more explicitly
addressed. The crucial distinction in relation to the discussion of cultural
facilities is whether the author of 'class-conscious' literature felt himself
to be writing as member of (a spokesman for) the proletariat, or as an
author in abstract who took working-class life or experience as a topic
(see Vicinus 1974 on working-class authors).

In the former case when authors are writing literature from a self-
conscious base in the proletariat, they are likely to be conscious of a duel
problem. First, the natural desire to get things right — to utilize their
access to 'privileged' knowledge of social life — raises a whole series of
issues about attitude, for example whether heroes should be heroes in
terms of bourgeois values or class heroes. And secondly, whether the
tools at hand 'indicate the fragile, almost vulnerable position of the
proletarian writer, who feels that he must try to register his human
experience in all its distinctive difference but is drawn irresistably before
the models of middle-class literary expression which are constantly before
him' (Johnson 1975 p.73). The second type of working-class literature is

more common, it includes all material in which the lives of the working class are either subject or the setting for the story. In this case the material is likely to be reporting 'unusual' features either with amusement, tolerance, horror or as a device for moral instruction. If we extend the category of literature to the extreme and include publications like collections of folk songs and street ballads etc., then we can get a very clear insight into a selective response to working-class life. Not only was politically unreliable material deleted but songs which were too bawdy might be thought inadvisable, and these selections were masked by a patronizing excessive use of dialect forms to indicate both authenticity and the 'quaintness' of proletarian customs (see the discussion of sources in Colls 1977). In a literature about the working class there might be some attempt to respond to the complexities of working-class attitudes and values, but the distancing involved in appropriating those insights as the 'stuff' of literary canons was too great and there was a conventional recourse to moralizing stereotypes.

I shall take as a second type of illustration of issues in proletarian literature the development of literature as novels in African societies (the academic literature is not as extensive in this case, for introductions to styles of African writing see Yale French Studies 1976; Soyinka 1976; for the cultural context of novels see Obiechina 1975; Mutiso 1974). I use the rather clumsy form of 'literature as novels' because although the writing and publication of indigenous novels from sub-Saharan Africa is a comparatively recent development, this does not mean that there is no literary culture. Rather it means that before the beginning of this century the literary culture was not designed for publication, but consisted largely of story-telling and modes of speech rich in proverbial and idiomatic allusion and reference. This cultural history has meant that the division noted above between authors who write about a popular audience and those who write from within that audience is particularly salient in relation to African literature. Even if we ignore the romantic tradition in which Africa is used as an exotic setting and only bear in mind those novelists who have attempted to capture realistically African experience, European writers are characteristically crippled by their inability to transcend cultural presuppositions. Obiechina (1975 p.26) points out that Africans in European novels usually speak European English while some West African authors 'by incorporating the oral tradition of West Africa into their writing . . . have largely succeeded in giving an air of authenticity to their writing and established a consciousness which is characteristically West African'. In such societies as the under-developed countries of Africa we have rapid urbanization allied with the investment of large sums in the acquisition of contemporary mass communication facilities, so that we would expect a fairly rapid decay of village 'folk' traditions in favour of more metropolitan popular art (it is in this sense that the audience is a proletariat if not a conventional working class), raising problems for artists of how to situate themselves *vis-à-vis* the emerging popular audience. A solution which has seemed to gain more prominence in French-speaking colonies than elsewhere in Africa is to emphasise a trans-structural cultural universal such as negritude (Betts 1971). An alternative understanding of the same theme has developed amongst African authors writing in English who have emphasized their role as guardians of a cultural heritage, who have self-consciously used aesthetic facilities to reconstitute cultural dignity.

This concern with dignity, with a recapitulation of cultural identity after the denigration of imperialism, recurs in the theoretical considerations of authors and propogandists in the third type of illustration. In the case of popular literature in post-revolutionary China the themes of cultural nationalism have been supplanted by a detailed consideration of the problems of constructing a revolutionary literature. In this case the problems turn around how to write proletarian literature from the standpoint of the proletariat while self-consciously reshaping the social order. In the previous examples a commitment to a proletarian standpoint has involved struggling with problems of documentary style, with grasping the ethnography of speech. Although this is true in the Chinese situation, so that in the canonical Talks at the Yenan Forum Mao Tsetung equates understanding the masses with learning the 'rich, lively language of the masses', Mao (1967 p.19) is very clear that a revolutionary standpoint involves transcending everyday experience in terms of what it ought to be: 'Life as reflected in works of literature and art can and ought to be on a higher plane, more intense, more concentrated, more typical, nearer the ideal, and therefore more universal than actual everyday life.' The way in which this process of simultaneous identification and transcendence becomes possible is through 'learning from the workers, peasants and soldiers'. Only by grasping the 'direction in which the proletariat is advancing' can revolutionary intellectuals understand the appropriate methods of creating a popular literature for a new society. The ability to grasp the direction of social change can only come from the masses themselves: 'China's revolutionary writers and artists, writers and artists of promise, must go among the masses; they must go for a long period of time unreservedly and wholeheartedly go among the masses of workers, peasants and soldiers, go into the heat of the struggle, go to the only source, the broadest and richest source, in order to observe, experience, study and analyse all the different kinds of people, all the classes, all the masses, all the vivid patterns of life and struggle, all the raw materials of literature and art. Only then can they proceed to do creative work' (*ibid*).

I believe that the self-conscious adaptation of popular art to the 'needs' of revolutionary social change can be particularly illuminating in relation to expectations for popular art by non-revolutionary authors. I will therefore continue to discuss some features of Chinese manifestos which develop the initial Maoist theses. I am of course aware that because popular art is taken seriously in Chinese politics manifestos are political tracts which express positions in struggles for power. Any full consideration would therefore have to situate the points made here in the context of political debates within and since the Cultural Revolution (cf. Fei-ling n.d.). A further complication derives from power struggles in the shifting political climate since Mao's death, I will therefore concentrate on themes developed by radical groups during the 1960s. The first point to be made is the importance which is attached to struggles about forms of popular expression. Forms of cultural expression are believed to be able to inspire individuals and to be able to encapsulate social change, so that not only are praiseworthy books particularly important but 'harmful' literature is more 'dangerous' the better it is. The intermeshing of literary and political values means that transforming art is in fact one of the most difficult tasks of the revolution: 'Can there possibly be any other old fortress that cannot be taken now that we have succeeded in taking the Fortress of Peking Opera which was under the strictest control of the counter-revolutionary revisionists and where the old forces were most stubborn?' (Chiang Ching 1968 p.11). But once it has been accomplished, i.e. the cultural implications of Mao's question 'who do we serve' have been grasped, then 'the more certain it is that no one will be able to match us in a war'.

The cultural implications, as fictional devices, of the political demands for popular art can be organized under three headings: a combination of revolutionary romanticism with revolutionary realism; anti-humanism; and anti-aesthetic. I will briefly illustrate each of these headings in turn. The first means that although proletarian art must be authentic in the sense of being based on proletarian experience, it should not aspire to be critically realistic; indeed it is a trait of revisionism to try to deflect attention from progressive romanticism. In an interview with the Chinese novelist Hao Jan he describes how a bourgeois rightist editor returned his early work because the editor believed one needed to 'expose the seamy side of life [in order to] produce important literature.' (*Hsinhua Weekly* Issue No. 224, 24 May 1973). The condemnation of humanism extends the meaning of revolutionary romanticism. In effect what is being attacked here is the use of psychological insight by the author to qualify the dramatic impact of events in the narrative. For example the Soviet novelist Sholokhov is severely criticized because he acknowledges that the losses sustained in a war, even a just war such as that against Nazi Germany, cause sadness which lingers after the war. Similarly, other detailed criticisms of revisionist work often point to the use of personal feelings, such as horror at the torture of relatives or the misery of enemies, as deflecting attention from the 'real' meaning of events and implying that there are human responses which are shared by all people regardless of social context. (Cavendish (1968 p.80) interestingly points out that the denial of humanism 'constitutes the most fundamental chasm between

the Chinese Communist approach and all varieties of liberalism.')
Revolutionary romanticism is therefore a progressive approach to aesthetic representation because it aspires to be exemplary, to overcome the
qualified understanding of revisionist knowledge, and to situate itself as
a 'noble image of proletarian heroes': 'Another Shensi-province peasant
artist, in explaining revolutionary realism and revolutionary romanticism,
pointed to Tung's painting which shows a net overflowing with a fish
of a stunning variety of colours: "There is such a pond on the commune,
and there are fish in it. That is the reality. But the number is not so great,
and the fish not so many-coloured as you see in the picture. That is what
it will be in the future" ' (Zaniello 1975 p.158). The final heading, anti-
aesthetics, refers to the rejection of most of the conventional devices of
aesthetic verisimilitude. Although some of the slogans are a little opaque
I believe that the following quotation from the summary of the *Forum
on Literature and Art* etc. (1968 p.7), gives a good idea of what are
seen as bourgeois ideas on literature and art: 'Typical expressions of this
line are such theories as those of "truthful writing", "the broad path to
realism", "the deepening of realism", opposition to "subject matter as the
decisive factor", "middle characters", opposition to the "smell of
gunpowder" and "the merging of various trends as the spirit of the age".'

These critical headings indicate what must be avoided, they point to
the deficiencies of revisionism but need to be elaborated by considering
what should be achieved. The central aspiration can be described as
formulating an exemplary aesthetic, so that, rather than recognizing the
qualifications of human ambivalence, proletarian art should embrace an
heroic style in which revolutionary protagonists do not vacillate, hesitate
or fear: 'We should centre our efforts mainly on writing about the bright,
on praising our great victories in socialist revolution and socialist reconstruction, that is, praising the triumph of Mao Tsetung's thought, on
presenting the world-shaking heroism and wisdom of proletarian revolutionary fighters in the struggle, on portraying the heroic workers, peasants
and soldiers of our era and not on presenting the 'good side' and the
'bad side' half and half' (Yao Wenyuan 1968 pp.26-7). It is recognized
that this approach is not a complete innovation but is based on the
dramatic style of traditional Peking Opera where characterization is very
stylized; the moral didacticism of the characterization is now intensified
and heightened (for a useful illustrated history of heroism in Chinese
communist fiction see Huang; see also the discussion of theatre in Snow
1972). The structural correlate of these theses is that an artist cannot
construct appropriate heroic models in the abstract but must distill them
from mass experience: this process has dual forms — authors learning
from the people, and the people utilizing their experience to become
authors. The basis of this structural practice can be found in the politics
of the Yenan base (see Selden 1971). Both aspects have been praised and
should encourage a populism which would temper the more arbitrary

aspects of an exemplary aesthetic: 'Workers, peasants and soldiers are now producing many fine philosophical articles which splendidly express Mao Tsetung's thought in terms of their own practice. . . . In particular, both in content and in form the numerous poems by workers, peasants and soldiers appearing on wall-newspapers and blackboards herald an entirely new age' (*Summary of the Forum* etc., *op. cit.* p.10). The difficulty with such cultural populism is that it cannot be allowed to be autonomous: 'As for the cadres in charge of creative work in literature and art, they should always bear two points in mind: First, be good at listening to the opinions of the broad masses; second, be good at analysing these opinions, accept the right ones and reject the wrong ones' (*op. cit.* p.16). Popular art can be politicized as can engineering but this does not mean that it is appropriate to draw an analogy between cultural intellectuals as experts and the technical expertise of engineers. The latter can be integrated into the production community through the exemplification of such slogans as being red and expert and putting politics in command. Cultural intellectuals not only lack the local policy unit as an entity to give meaning to their work, but are simultaneously asked to play an articulating role between the locality and the ideological centre. This contradiction in the concept of an intelligentsia and its modes of production is magnified by a revolutionary culture which has an exemplary aesthetic but lacks a form other than stylized romanticism.

I have been trying to elucidate the argument that producing popular art, as with any other type of art, involves the author situating himself *vis-à-vis* his audience — situate to be understood in two senses: the first is the authority to create an acceptable fiction and the second is his understanding of the boundaries of his fiction in relation to the realities of the world of his audience. In both senses the character of the choices the author makes will express the sort of community envisaged as content for that work. I have tried to illustrate the process by taking the general example of proletarian literature, in particular working-class literature in nineteenth-century Britain, indigenous novels in urbanizing African societies, and exemplary art in revolutionary Chinese society. I have discussed the last example in greater detail because it involves some fairly clear expectations about the constitutive power of popular art. Of course I am not in a position to evaluate the popularity of the art produced, it is claimed that it is eagerly endorsed by the masses (although the same claim is made for work produced by Lew Grade), nor is it appropriate for me to evaluate aesthetic quality, although from that available to us in Western Europe it does seem excrutiatingly dull and lacking in any sort of imaginative vigour. What does seem clear is that the transformation from folk tradition to popular art in contemporary China (although by now well out of date and uneven in quality, see the collection of material edited by Crozier (1970) on this transformation), involves a distinct reworking of what I called above opportunities for constitutive participation in modes of representation. At its best the forms of imaginative expression which were developed became part of the politics of everyday experiences: 'The distinction between "life" and "drama" became less acute in all these manifestations of revolution but nowhere more so than in the struggle meetings. . . . In them was a strong element of carnival, as in the almost daily local street parades announcing news with gongs and cymbals . . . of spectacle, as in the huge meetings parading top officials in public stadiums; and of drama' (Howard 1971 p.80).

The process of reworking opportunities for constitutive participation practically parallels the aesthetic concerns of many in the West European avant garde this century, for example, a rejection of tradition, of cultural history, as a stifling weight; secondly, a concern with methods of fictive representation (the means by which people are 'drawn into' the performance) — in practice this has meant a common rejection of naturalism as an aesthetic method; thirdly, a common concern to transcend the distinction between life and drama so that spectacles are politicized and dramatic events become 'happenings' which disrupt conventional expectations (a celebration of cultural anarchy); and finally, a common belief that social and cultural revolutions both require and are constituted through cataclysmic change. In drawing these parallels I am not oblivious to the fact that any suggestion that there was a common purpose between European avant garde decadence and art in Chinese society would be deeply offensive to the Chinese, but I wish to bring out the argument that revolutionizing popular art involves as radical reconsideration of the role of the producer as any other aesthetic transformation. The history of the avant garde in Europe in this century allows us to see that aesthetic innovation provides for a limited set of practical options: there are, first, those who restrict their innovations to the exploration of formal problems (in practice this sort of restriction is almost impossible to sustain, but if one were looking for paradigmatic examples I would think of figures like Mondrian or Schoenberg); a second option is to explore innovations as they contribute to our conceptions of the everyday environment, and in this sense such innovators are transforming perceptual categories (at its best, work under this heading should come under the third option, for example some aspects of work associated with the Bauhaus, but I am thinking of innovations like New York Abstract Expressionism which has contributed to a rethinking of public style); finally, a third option is to query the boundaries of the socio-cultural conventions which demarcate fictional experience, and thereby bring into question the relationship between stance as author and the form of expression of the fiction (dadaism and surrealism).

It is because some strands in avant-garde innovation have questioned structural relationships that elitist experimentation has often claimed to be a new 'popular' art, so that the most complex experiments in contemporary jazz have often been seen by their authors as rethinking popular experience within the black community. I have argued that in revolutionary China the intelligentsia have formulated an exemplary aesthetic of stultifying romanticism as a solution to the problems involved in creating a popular art that was both authentic and inspirational. I do not believe this is the only possible solution, and as a concluding illustration of the relationships between the social organization of cultural production and form of expression I shall briefly discuss the development of a prescriptive aesthetic amongst the intelligentsia in the first decade of the Russian revolution, with particular reference to the theatre in the first decade of the revolution. In essence, a prescriptive aesthetic may be defined as the attempt to utilize the devices of fictional articulation as ways of defamiliarizing conventions of knowledge, as a means of transcending the distinctions between life and drama to construct new modes of participation. In this aesthetic, crafts, for example, are seen as styles of social participation rather than vessels to be filled with politically appropriate content (as illustrations of the latter approach see the disastrous Chinese folk arts such as paper-cuts or songs which have been taken over wholesale and given new titles or new topics).

The first point to be made is that in trying to make a theatre for the people revolutionary artists were attracted by the concept of spectacle as the dramatic staging of extraordinary experience. The idea of a spectacle as a breathtaking event to be marvelled at is obviously rooted in the festival traditions of peasant experience, but after the revolution spectacles were adapted to new political purposes to provide a forum for staging important events (such as the famous reenactment of the storming of the Winter Palace in 1920), or to provide a highly stylized interpretation of epic moments in proletarian history — a parallel is to think of such spectacles as *tableaux vivants* on a mass scale (Deak 1975). The motif of spectacle was congenial to revolutionary art because it combined two strands: the first was an emphasis upon the theatre as celebration, the absence of a conventional theatrical tradition amongst the proletariat could be filled by providing a utopian theatre in which the people were the authors enacting a new politics: 'The future theatre will be formed from elements of physical culture, joy, simplicity, sunniness, valour and impulses towards common brotherly universal unification.' (Meyerhold quoted in Barooshian 1975 p.106). Secondly, the stylization of character and narrative structure in spectacular presentations meant that this type of theatre was consistent with other innovations in politicization such as agit-prop trains and boats touring the countryside, and travelling film units showing Kino-Pravda news shorts, and other types of poster and display, which were all attempting to mobilize enthusiasm for the new social order. (For further discussion of the relationships between the arts and the new political order see Fitzpatrick, 1970; Gray 1970.) Spectacles in urban centres were organized through a simple structure of montage in which the 'action' shifted from distinct stages, such as different parts of a square or even off the square as when battleships provided appropriate blasts. The significant elaboration of this form was that the 'audience' was included as an element in the staging. In terms of performances which took place within a theatre this was accomplished by mingling cast and audience, by interrupting the action with 'real' reports on developments in the civil war, by breaking up the stage into a number of levels, and by rendering stage design through abstract forms. Such innovations completely undercut the illusions of naturalistic theatre because: 'Meierkhol'd believed that estrangement and deformation of theatrical forms would evoke a new perception, if not a new illusion, of the theatre' (Barooshian *op. cit.* p.109).

Revolutionary theatre in Russia, as in the other arts, was therefore being used to combine the aesthetic innovations of the avant garde (even to the extent of claiming that the political revolution was an expression of aesthetic imperatives), with the socio-structural changes inherent in overturning the established social order. Amongst the features of avant-garde innovation which were adopted and adapted for performances for the new popular art were: irreverence, both for established expressive forms and as a response to topics; a style of work which came to be labelled eccentrism for the stylization of actors' expressions and for the lack of clear narrative structure; a 'cinematic' juggling with reality, so called because of the salience of montage discussed above and because the aspects of the story presented were governed by directorial desires rather than provided by the logic of the scene portrayed; and documentarism, an idea used here in two senses, first, the disruption of actor and audience divisions in which the idea of a chorus as representing the people became popular, and secondly a style of factography in which the theatre was used to obliterate distinctions between drama (fiction) and social facts. A linking theme in these aesthetic innovations is a recurrent emphasis upon the making of a work of art so that the 'art-ness' of aesthetic experience was held to be found in participation rather than in a finished object. The aesthetic innovations of the Constructivists found common cause with the critical insights of the Formalists in arguing that reality could not be a copy of what is but a revelation of how it came to be: 'This new attitude to·objects in which, in the last analysis, the object becomes more perceptible, is that artificiality which, in our opinion, creates art. . . . The artistic . . . is created expressly to liberate perception from automatism and that the aim of the artist is the "seeing" ' (Shklovsky 1974 pp.114-5).

This approach provides a radical challenge to the exemplary aesthetic developed in China, it offers an alternative prescriptive aesthetic in which authors who saw themselves responding to a political and social imperative sought for ways of reconstructing experience through the destruction of conventional expressive imagery. This programme, prescription, involves moving from art as privileged experience to art as everyday practice: 'The programme of Constructivism aimed at the overthrow of the

division between utility, artistic pursuits and free expression — between
the unique and duplicated work, . . . It was Rodchenko who elevated mass
printing — book covers and ordinary brochures, the wrappers of poor
quality sweets, newspaper advertisements, labels and film leaders — to the
rank of genuine graphic art' (Bojko 1972 p.25). Thus one version of the
slogans of the Constructivists was: '1 Down with art. Long live technic.
2 Religion is a lie. Art is a lie. 3 Kill human thinking's last remains tying it
to art. 4 Down with guarding the traditions of art. Long live the
Constructivist technician. 5 Down with art which only camouflages
humanity's impotence. 6 The collective art of the present is constructive
life' (quoted in Bann 1974 p.20). The central difference between an
exemplary aesthetic and a prescriptive aesthetic is therefore a different
conception of work. In revolutionary popular art in China the performance
remains the work, so that despite the emphasis upon popular participation
and learning from the people the audience is presented with an essentially
finished aesthetic experience. The Futurist alternative as articulated in
revolutionary Russia was an attempt to develop an aesthetic on construction in which the making of the performance was the work. The explanation of the difference is located in the relative autonomy of the intelligentsia in the different societies, and the innovations of the Russian avant
garde were effectively suppressed when Party hegemony was established
because: 'The Party therefore felt, paradoxically, much safer with the
a-political theatrical traditionalists, whose aesthetic orientation was far
more attuned to that of the Bolshevik leaders' (Barooshian *op. cit.*
p.113). The significance of authors' aspirations is that the forms of
popular art are dynamic constructs which involve serious political
questions about the collectivity which is being constituted through the
performance.

Popular Narratives

The cumulative argument of the first two parts of this chapter is that an
important dimension of a story's significance derives from the way the
story has been put together. More specifically, the story's presuppositions
about the relationships between author, audience and community constitute a 'vision' or 'perspective', a way of structuring the story, which
relates to institutionalized relationships in the social context. It is this
'rhetorical code' which expresses the distinctive understanding of society
available in fictional experience. In the concluding part of the chapter I
shall continue the discussion of fictions and attempt to show how there
is a correspondence between narrative structure and the relations of
fictional production.

In the course of the overall discussion I have noted several characteristic features of popular art. First, a concern with narrative tension — the
performance is constructed to narrate a story so that the audience is

concerned about the outcome. This is not meant to indicate that popular narratives are unpredictable, very often the opposite is the case, but that the predictability does not preclude dramatic tension. Secondly, there is a characteristic concern with narrative realism, these concepts are becoming rather over-used but they summarize well the ways in which details are tellingly used to authenticate and contextualize the main dramatic work. This has meant that although much popular art is fantastic or stylized beyond any attempt at 'realistic' characterization (for example films by the Marx Brothers), such horrors or comedies are still governed by conventions of character and setting; and thereby the stories told become parables for considerably more routine experience. Thirdly, another characteristic feature is the extravagance of the performance, the ways in which the most flea-bitten fair or cheapest production will aspire to the aura of the spectacular. Of course some performances take this aura as their central *raison d'être* and are celebrated for the extravagance of their staging (*Gone with the Wind* and *Cleopatra*), but in such cases another related feature of the spectacle becomes clearer — this is what I will call the desire for vicarious authenticity. In such cases the spectacular provides an opportunity for a member of an audience to participate in and yet be distanced from someone risking his life crossing the Niagara Falls, an organization spending many millions of pounds, and Christians actually being eaten by lions etc. Finally, the performance of the story is usually reassuringly predictable. The crowds pouring into a football ground are not just spectators, they are celebrants at a rite of communal identification. Secular ceremonials display a method of representation or portraiture but they also ritualize themselves — they assert a dignity in everyday experience. These features are both characteristic and distinctive of popular cultural experience; they provide the terms in which a narrative vision can be expressed.

In order to get an initial grasp of how these characteristic features provide a distinctive perspective it is appropriate to discuss film as a paradigm of popular entertainment. For example, it is possible to read Georg Lukacs's *The Meaning of Contemporary Realism* as drawing on a root metaphor of a theatrical conception of reality. By theatrical I mean here a picture-stage version of dramatism in which the audience is outside the action, watching it unfold and critically evaluating the performances of individuals. Although the work of art is determined by the use of perspective and selection for Lukacs the principles of selection must derive from the 'facts of the case': 'But literature must have a concept of the normal if it is to 'place' distortion correctly; that is to say, to see it *as* distortion' (1963 p.33). I describe such a confident sense of normality as theatrical because the picture-stage brackets the performance, a member of the audience is not required to query the normality of his observational stance; and because the association of bourgeois propriety implicit in nineteenth-century theatrical idioms seems most appropriate for Lukacs' stuffy distaste for pathologies. Film provides an alternative root metaphor in that the nature of filmic dramatization overrides theatrical distancing and constitutes an account of social action which is inherently modernistic — in Lukacs's terms. The nature of reality portrayed in filmic performances provides such an alternative because of the structural principle of montage. This works in two ways, first, because the camera effectively supplants our eyes as the medium of perception and yet the camera cannot act as if it were a character (it soon becomes very boring if we are limited to what one person would have seen), therefore the camera accumulates identity by continually shifting between viewpoints; and secondly, because meaning is accumulated through the conjunction of images — for example the meaning of a facial expression is clarified by the way it is succeeded by an image which indicates the object of his expression. Montage provides for film to become meaningful through the associations between metaphors, there is no necessary restriction of space or time and the 'objectivity' of the reality that is being constituted cannot be taken for granted: 'In the works of Kafka, Beckett and Robbe-Grillet the environment becomes known to the reader only according to the narrating consciousness, . . . The fiction therefore is the "thing itself" ' (Szanto 1972 pp.8 and 12).

I am not arguing that films must inevitably represent modernist subjectivism rather than critical realism (there are films which are uncontroversially critical realist, for example the work of Jean Renoir), nor that films cannot be naturalist (naive documentarism often tries to avoid what Grierson called the 'artifice' of Hollywood), but that the organization of story-telling in filmic dramatization requires the spectator to participate in making sense so that the real context for the story is displayed through the story. In saying that the film has a paradigmatic status as a medium of popular entertainment I do more than repeat that cinematic performances are the most internationally common form of entertainment, certainly commercial entertainment, I argue that the nature of filmic dramatization captures most clearly the characteristic concerns of a popular aesthetic. It would be easy enough to point to films which illustrate the concerns of narrative tension, narrative realism, spectacular extravagance and ceremonial as they have been briefly described above: in particular because these headings related to the discussion of subjective involvement that I have identified as a consequence of montage. Although in all media there are no accidental features, that is characters only say, act, do, appear etc., as they do because the author(s) have so decided, in most performances there is an implicit distinction between foreground and background so that the latter provides a context for the dramatic action of the former. In film this distinction is centrally important because what I have called narrative realism often depends upon features of background and yet of course nothing appears in the final print without the authorization of the producers. It is in this sense that film provides for a total control of the reality it constitutes while seeming to mimic features of everyday experience. The popular aesthetic of film is therefore an infinite engagement with the boundaries of fiction and reality — we are continually negotiating our position *vis-à-vis* the story being told.

Richardson (1969 p.11) has argued that film is the paradigmatic medium of artistic expression for the machine age because, amongst other reasons, film is peculiarly appropriate through its technical complexity and because film provides for collaborative working on aesthetic experience which recaptures the inspired artisanship of medieval gothic: 'The film, like the cathedral, is one of those rare arts which . . . reflect, in broad and general ways, . . . the spirit of a whole age, because its appeal is at last not to the specialist, but to every man'. A more technical analysis can be adapted from Grant's (1970) distinction between conscientious and conscious realisms. The former is essentially a naturalistic aspiration to record the facts of the case inspired by a belief in the appropriateness of science as a model of intellectual endeavour. The latter, conscious realism, grew out of doubts about the reliability of empirical materials and of an increasing concern with the means of perception and representation: ' . . . realism in its conscious phase depends upon an awareness of its own complexity' (*op. cit.* p.70). The distinction between these styles of realism obviously parallels a distinction between naturalism and modernism, but it may also help us to grasp the significance of film aesthetics. The film image implies an unproblematic naturalism in recording its subject and yet a probing subjectivism in constructing a narrative, and therefore film can be seen as a synthesis of both types of realism. (It may be because some films veer too closely to either pole of naturalism or subjectivism that they lose any hope of a popular audience.) An understanding of film as synthetic, in this sense, is also consistent with Richardson's argument that film is 'an extension of the older narrative arts' (for example he reminds us of Eisenstein's remark that Griffiths derived the idea of montage from Dickens (p.17)). Filmic discourse can be seen therefore to be extending the languages of story-telling.

I have suggested that film embodies a perspective in story-telling which is particularly appropriate for the characteristic features of popular aesthetic. This concept of perspective has also been referred to as a language for story-telling or narrative structure. In order to elucidate these concepts, although by a complete contrast, we can turn to the interesting illustration of the significance of changes in kinds of story-telling, which comes in the humanistic developments summarized as the Twelth-Century Renaissance. In several arts the nature of governing narrative forms were questioned and changed in ways that were consistent with an argument 'discoveries about the nature and possibilities of narrative may, perhaps must, take place at times when there are in progress

revaluations of much larger cultural scope, but that the discoveries themselves are about narrative, and are not necessarily of a character that
connects them in an obvious way with the changes that accompany
them' (Kermode 1972 p.9). The shift in narrative form from epic to
romance in the course of the twelth-century articulated a new way of
presuming narrative relevance, a new relationship of author and audience,
and a cognitive significance to the story being told. To illustrate briefly
each of these claims in turn: by narrative relevance I mean the assumption
that we have since come to take for granted that the participants in a
story have to be described in a way that makes sense of their actions in
the story: 'The marriage of matter and meaning, of narrative and commentary, was the key to the new kind of narrative poetry — the poetry
that assumed in the reader both the ability and the desire to think of an
event in terms of what one's mind could build upon it' (Vinaver 1971
p.23). It seems to me that Schapiro's (1973 chp. 4) discussion of the
contemporary shift from frontal to profile as symbolic forms of a mode
of development and characterization reinforces this point. The new
relationship between author and audience is inherent in changing expectations of the reader but was also shown in the development of vernacular
writings which the audience was expected to read rather than listen to
being read. Thirdly, the cognitive significance of the story refers to the
implicit parallels between the structure of the story being told (the
narrative order), and the conceptual shape of the events and relationships
which constitute the story. Once again this point is perhaps hard to grasp
because we take the orderliness of narrative and experience for granted;
which is not to say that the order must be self-evident but that the new
developments can be woven into the logic of the narrative structure:
'. . . each initial adventure can be extended into the past and each final
adventure into the future by a further lengthening of the narrative
threads' (Vinaver *op. cit.* p.76).

The concept of perspective in fictional experience is therefore being
used to refer to a level of dramatic organization implicit in the story
being told or enacted. A useful way of formulating the concept is
provided by Chatman's distinction between *story* as 'the what is being
depicted' and *discourse* as the 'how' of expression (1975). It is not necessary to recapitulate Chatman's discussion, but the concept of narrative
as semiotic 'that is, meaning-bearing in its own right', a form of expression
analytically distinguishable from the form of content is attractively consistent with my thesis that significant experience is constituted through
the organization of narrative relationships. If ' "Narrative statement" and
"to state narratively" are thus meant as technical terms for any expression
of a narrative element viewed independently of its manifesting substance'
(Chatman *op. cit.* p.309), then we are beginning to formulate a technical
vocabulary for 'reading' performances 'independently of the intention or
instruction of the author who is therefore neither the source of a message

nor an authority on reading. All narratives are like this.' (Kermode *op. cit.* p.15). I realize that the great majority of those concerned with issues in narrative analysis are dealing with topics 'inside' the performance; for example, the ways in which the imaginative illusion of the change of time is carried off by narrative materials that are static and temporally limited. (Besides the references to particular essays I have also been interested in collections such as those edited by Chatman, 1973; Bloomfield, 1970; and *New Literary History*.) But if we are going to work with ideas of 'stating narratively' then we do not have to restrict our analysis to the 'language' or 'code' of stating but can conceptualize the articulation as a mode of social discourse — a mode of practical interaction.

The conventions of stating narratively must be essential for the story to appear adequate, and yet the distinction between story and discourse tends to be invisible in the course of story-telling: 'So much are we *in* the narrative that in normal reading we tend to disregard the medium' (Chatman p.302). Our work in constituting the joins between story elements is a procedural requirement that we take for granted because we have already accepted that a certain type of performance is taking place. To put this another way, although montage in film narratives is a crucial mode of stating narratively it depends upon a sophistication amongst the audience that has to be learnt and developed. As Kermode (*op. cit.* p.20) notes, the practice of self-conscious reading demands that 'the reader . . . must forget how he used to read, deluded by local and provincial restrictions; . . . and instead develop the creative activity which narrative always demands in some measure, but which may be deadened by over-familiarity and by trained expectations too readily satisfied.' In the course of her thoughtful essays on the nature of fictive discourse Barbara Herrnstein-Smith (1976 p.40) has emphasized that poetic meanings are not exchanged by speaker-hearers as natural utterances but are inscribed as fictive utterances: 'For the utterance that it [the poem] represents to be experienced as meaningful, a plausible context for it must be constructed by the reader.' Thus the process of interpreting or reading is the activity of providing a context, of resituating the performance in a different social milieu. If this were not so an authoritative interpretation of performance, meaning could be reached through asking the author(s) for a paraphrase, or through a critical consensus that would be fixed for all audiences. Instead of course: 'The language of a poem continues to mean as long as we have meanings to provide for it. Its meanings are exhausted only at the limits of the reader's own experience and imagination' (Herrnstein-Smith 1971 p.278). The narrative which forms expression, utterance or performance, may therefore be understood as an invitation, a proposal to invest sense with significance.

It is characteristic of our intellectual culture that the idea of an invitation in fictional form is likely to be thought an abstract possibility — something to be inferred by critical insight. An alternative interpretation

is that the invitation is more situationally rooted, it is expressed through
the occasion of performance: 'Moving from the neat confines of the
narrative text, we confront the performance as a totality encompassing
not only the verbal story but the entire narrative experience, auditory and
visual, of spectator and actor' (Colby and Peacock p.624). The central
illustrative resource for Peacock's reflections on the status of symbolic
action is his own study of the role of a type of Indonesian proletarian
drama, *ludruk,* in helping 'persons symbolically define their movements
from one type of situation to another — from traditional to modern situations' (1968 p.6). *Ludruk* is a type of dramatic spectacle which is proletarian in that it is performed in rather ramshackle surroundings for
working-class audiences and it is extremely popular; it is also proletarian
in that at least some *ludruk* troupes were involved in working-class politics
and associated with communist factions (these remarks are based on
Peacock's study which was substantially completed before the anti-
communist massacres of the mid-1960s). I do not have sufficient space to
report in detail on Peacock's sensitive responses to shifts in plot structure,
characterization, satirical interruptions and songs etc., but he uses all
this material to develop an account of *ludruk* as a buffer between the
'Western' commercial entertainment of the urban centres and traditionalist
'folk' dramas. Some instances of headings he uses to indicate the enactment of rites of modernization are: specialization — the development of
specialist agencies catering for social needs outside the household or
kampung in which *ludruk* offers impersonal entertainment; centralization
— *ludruk* acts as rites of national identity through a more uniform
popular culture and thereby provides a medium of mental exchange for
the heterogeneous social encounters of urban life; rationalization — a
process in which animistic or folk magic elements are undervalued to be
replaced by a public rationality or means-ends schemas, although Peacock
realizes that *ludruk* may not be rigorously rational but may endorse change
by holding up the positive features of modernity. These processes help
to elucidate the social role of proletarian drama, although the features
of dramatic performance used as illustrative resources are not treated as
discrete elements but as parts of a narrative which signifies through its
formulaic power for participants: 'I have stressed that the melodrama,
by musical climax, narrative movement, passage imagery, and other formal
devices lures *ludruk* participants into joining a motion towards particular
experiences . . . and that by getting involved in such motions the participants learn to act and orient towards the world in certain ways (such as
lineally, continuously, innovatively)' (*op. cit.* p.245).

The idea of occasion as a distinct area of cultural space for types of
story-telling may be developed in two ways. First, as a physical space as
when a building becomes a church or shrine in which physical metaphors,
that have acquired autonomy and become abstracted from their initial
referent and thereby have become symbols, are stored; these symbols

encapsulate narratives and are used to heighten the solemnity of narrative enactment. Secondly, as temporal space when narrators 'breakthrough into performance' in Hymes's (1975) phrase, and use tale-telling opportunities as enactments of traditional commitments and identities. In either case the occasion will be marked by a ceremonial solemnity on the part of participants. In practice it is useful to distinguish between interactive and operative ceremonies (Skorupski 1976 in particular chaps. 6 and 7). The former are those 'strips' of formal interaction in which it is the existence of a code that is being ceremonially marked. Thus when we greet others, acknowledge the implications of a style of dress, join in a supporters' chant, we are emphasizing that a code is in operation, i.e. that there is an orderliness to the interaction, and that we are appropriate participants in those actions: 'Thus formality is associated with *gravitas*, a sense of one's own worth and social autonomy' (*op. cit.* p.88). Operative ceremonies are part of the same category in that they mark something out as proper and as socially on record but differ in that they provide for the accomplishment of 'new patterns of rules' and thereby new statuses and new institutions. An operative ceremony is more likely to be liminal: 'Simpler societies seem to feel that only a person temporarily without status, property, rank, or office is fit to receive the tribal gnosis or occult wisdom which is in effect knowledge of what the tribes people regard as the deep structure of culture and indeed of the universe' (Turner 1973 p.241). It is on such occasions, when the certitude of everyday experience is deliberately suspended, that a narrative as a performance which in its saying or doing accomplished the unsayable is likely to take on central cultural significance (cf. Lawson 1976). The intermingling of narrative and ceremonial on this occasion may take off from the confines of the initial rite and become generalized as a festival in which the inversion of the social order is celebrated.

The significance of ceremonial in theatrical experience is a key element in Schechner's discussion of the poetics of performance (1976). He too has drawn heavily on Turner's work on the boundaries of conventional cultural space and the status of pilgrimages as physical metaphors for participation. Schechner argues that carnivals in ceremonial centres are the basis of theatrical experience in that they involve transforming physical space to cultural text by writing on it, that is, by accumulating ceremonial lore and imagery so that space becomes an opportunity for performance. An emphasis upon making theatre as transformation of space implies that journeying to that space is inherent in the theatrical experience: 'The pattern of gathering, performing, dispersing is one which I call the basic theatrical pattern' (*op. cit.* p.44). Formulating the theatrical pattern in this way it is apparent that it need not be 'staged' but could occur 'naturally' as in a street accident, so that a further performance becomes necessary when the events are dramatically re-staged in a court-room. Traditional or ceremonial theatre is 'transformational' in that 'Just as a farm is a field where edible foods are grown, so a theatre is a place where transformations of time, place, and persons (human and non-human) are accomplished' (*op. cit.* p.49), then it is an appropriate metaphor that contemporary theatre tends to be staged as carefully bounded opportunities for transformation in state-licensed (funded) 'art fortresses'. In such circumstances 'the play' is a dramatic event which provides a vicarious transformation for the audience, but the social drama of theatrical experience in which both actors and audience are participants is organized so that the narrative ceases to be transformative and the occasion is neutralized by formulae of national entertainment.

The most common objection to arguments in which a connection is drawn between the ritual ceremonies of tribal societies and the perform-ances of contemporary popular entertainment, is that the narratives of the former deal with significant items of cultural consciousness, such as origin myths, while the narratives of the latter deal with relatively trivial issues in domestic or occupational experience. This comparison is irrelevant because one can argue that in a heterogeneous society it is not the form of particular items that is significant, but the ways in which those items can be seen to share an underlying form, a narrative structure. An intriguing and original attempt to explore an aesthetic order as it structured social reality is developed in Kinser and Kleinman's (1969) study of German history in the first half of this century. An aesthetic order is the form which provides for the sensibility of meanings in social experience: 'The mythic, like any statement, organizes meaning by highlighting and shaping details and by arranging them into a declarative plot. A myth explains the past, the present and the future, and its narrative shape establishes its historical reliability — or at least that is its purpose' (*op. cit.* p.12). The organization of meaning is implicit, it is provided in materials by continu-ities of style, topic, connotation and angle of view etc. The authors find non-verbal material particularly appropriate for their purposes because such material is essentially declarative — it works through form so that: 'non-verbal meaning is not communicated, as we often assume meaning must be, through the accumulation and logical connection of sequences and ideas. The operating principle at work here is: "We are what we do" ' (*op. cit.* p.17). It is impossible effectively to summarize their analysis of formal imagery without reproducing their instances, but the effective weight of their approach can be conveyed by grasping the attempt to transfer the distinction between story and discourse to the level of a language of cultural style.

The level of form I have called stating narratively has been described as a process of transformation, in which either sites or occasions or images are adapted to make an invitation to reconsider their use. This level of form is therefore providing an opportunity for a different type of social interaction. For example, the occasion of a religious festival may become celebrated by re-enacting the events the festival celebrates. This dramatization may be taken out of the original sacred site and be performed in its own right in the vernacular. Such an adaptation of the occasion provides an opportunity for a different mode of interaction, in this case becoming a member of an audience. Of course 'levels of form' do not provide opportunities in themselves but only through human activity, they are expressed through the ways in which fictional experience is produced and staged. The implication is that some ways of producing fictional experience will be organized so that narrative structures preclude important dimensions of fictional affect (the semantics of human relations). For example, the methods of funding and staging of national theatres, operas, art collections (in Russia circuses), is itself a mode of discourse in which the spectacle being performed is technically magnificent but essentially abstracted into being about spectacle itself. And this of course is the way one describes pornography — a way of producing fiction in which stories of sexual relationships may involve spectacular dimensions, but the rationale for the performance is that it can be endlessly restaged. In formulating narrative as a level of story-telling which structures the significance of fictional experience, I have been arguing that narratives structure through the organization of productive relationships which they articulate. I am therefore formulating an argument that is consistent with the themes of earlier chapters, — that the dialectic of interdependence between modes of social production and social consciousness as exemplified in fictional self-consciousness is mediated through narrative forms.

In order to illustrate this argument I shall turn to a paper by Philip Fisher (1975) in which he discusses the cultural significance of museums in contemporary culture. Fisher's paper is important because he provides an unusual insight into the relationship between narrative and story as we have conceptualized those terms, and because his work may help to elucidate my remark that contemporary 'high' culture is analogous in aesthetic stance to pornography. The development of museums immediately presents itself as a concern for aesthetic excellence, a retrieval of resources for the general good, but it may also be understood as part of a process through which the society reconceptualizes itself: 'From the mid-eighteenth century on, a point of intersection comes into being between new institutions and structures, the invention of museums and histories of art, new spatial arrangements of objects, a new historical sequencing that resocializes the European past by permitting it to rename itself art history' (*op. cit.* p.588). From this perspective museums mark a transformation of access, in the terms that have been used so far in this section the narrative organization of the multitudinous 'stories' which fill the shelves of museums, so that the objects are re-contextualized and given a different existential significance. We take it for granted that it would be inappropriate to worship an icon preserved in a gallery and the logic of that assumption must be that we are now members of a different public. That is, that the organization of the public changes the narrative structure of context, so that the narrative bespeaks *both* new stories and new institutional relationships: 'The museums locate for us one stage in the creation of new forms both of the assembly of objects and of the collective itself in social life — as new and deeply rooted in the realities of the new order as "the mob" ' (*op. cit.* p.589).

The transformation of access means that on the one hand objects lose their existential reference, ceremonial robes no longer help to constitute a ceremony, instead they become instances of new analytic schemes — periodization, stylistic analysis and genres. On the other hand, members of the public through their membership of an audience for such objects help to perpetuate an historical consciousness, a palpable civilization. In both cases the shift in aesthetic stance is away from occasion and from being physically grounded and towards an abstract socio-cultural essence. It is in this way that Malraux's conception of a museum without walls becomes more comprehensible — an infinite cultural space constituted by art in which the society is the invisible hand that silently arranged the style. Fisher points to instances of galleries with open walls, paradigmatically the Guggenheim museum, as a physical organization of space to articulate infinite space. Once this ideology of infinite inclusion has become established then contemporary performances are patronized to the extent that the museum directors etc., can feel confident that they will come to be seen as appropriate members of a scheme of historical style. In this framework objects can have no intrinsic value except as instances of the class they purport to constitute and thus their value is only determined by professionals. The controversy over national galleries, such as the Tate, buying 'meaningless' work, such as the bricks organized by Carl Andre, is incomprehensible to both professionals and public because neither side can appreciate that the other has a completely different perspective; the public look for objects meaningful in themselves while professionals look for objects which are meaningful through being instances of a schema. Finally, the one group who will be particularly sensitive to the transformation of access and its implications for the stories they are making are the producers. They are forced to explore the narrative which grounds or structures each content and with themselves as exploiters of these resources: 'Painting since Manet, literature since Flaubert and Baudelaire are reflective, self-conscious, deeply historical in inspiration, defiantly concerned with the grounds of art itself, in search of the minimal conditions of art,' (*op. cit.* p.603; it is interesting in this context to read Peter Gay's (1976) discussion of Manet's position *vis-à-vis* the development of 'modernism', although Gay criticizes the interpretations of Manet as revolutionary he agrees with Fisher that his innovations derived from an enormous concern with tradition).

It may be helpful at this point to recapitulate some features of the argument. From the distinction between narrative and story I have described the relationship between these levels of fiction as structural. The narrative structures the story that can be told, the performance that can be accomplished. From this point two implications have been deduced. The first is that a narrative can structure a story so that in an important sense it becomes meaningless; certain types of performance have a surface comprehensibility but seem to preclude the development their own story might initiate. The second is that in certain institutional contexts a narrative self-consciousness can develop so that producers of performances, story-tellers, increasingly investigate the possibilities which narratives provide for fictional expression. The rationality of narrative self-conscious-ness is that authors or producers cease to see themselves as completely autonomous in determining what their work will be 'about', but instead see their activity as an invitation: 'The end of art is to give a sensation of the object as seen, not as recognized. The technique of art is to make things "unfamiliar", to make forms obscure, so as to increase the difficulty and the duration of perception. The act of perception in art is an end in itself and must be prolonged. *In art it is our experience of the process of construction that counts, not the finished product*' (Shklovsky quoted in Scholes 1974 pp.83-4). From this perspective the sense of work in work of art is shifted from standing for an object and taken back to its more literal meaning as standing for an investment of human labour. Fictional experience must be worked through as the organization of collaborative relationships, so that meaning is something that becomes possible through differences in constitutive relationships. We can call this aesthetic perspec-tive constructivist because it entails an emphasis on the making of meaning. In attempting to reconsider some problems in Wittgenstein's later theory of semantics Gordon Baker (1974 pp.173-4) has argued that the essence of Wittgenstein's position can be captured by the slogan: 'If you want to discover what a sentence means, ask yourself "How could I know it?"; . . . the type of semantics that results from this basic principle I shall call Constructivism.'

   The relationship between constructivism and popular art is that because popular culture is embedded in lived experience, the narrative structure of formulaic art involves the members of the audience in maintaining an aesthetic distance from the spectacle. The entertainments of community life were parables of routine experience transformed through self-conscious and elaborate artifice: 'This effort to make the incidents represented appear strange to the public can be seen in a primitive form in the theatrical and pictorial displays at the old popular fairs' (Brecht in Willett 1963 p.91). The move from the artifice of play to the consumption of leisure as commodity has been part of a transformation of social and economic relationships, so that 'naive' formulas are now unlikely to be found. This does not preclude, however, the possibility that there can be a self-conscious exploration of narrative artifice in order to reconstruct fictional experience as popular aesthetic. And this of course is what Brecht attempted in his use of techniques of distancing and alienation: 'A representation that alienates is one which allows us to recognize its subject, but at the same time makes it seem unfamiliar. . . . Here is the outlook, disconcerting but fruitful, which the theatre must provoke with its representations of human social life. It must amaze its public' (*op. cit.* p.192). The link between formalist theories of constructivist aesthetics and Brechtian theatrical practice is, as are the other parallels in this argument, not fortuitous but an association of which the participants were aware, (cf. the papers by Mitchell and Brewster, 1974). Brechtian theatre is therefore epic (or spectacular), because it treats its own performance as a cause for wonder: 'The supreme task of an epic production is to give expression to the relationship between the action being staged and everything that is involved in the act of staging *per se*' (Benjamin 1973 p.11). The spectacle is inverted and ceases to be vicarious not by becoming more 'real' but by inviting the audience to participate actively in the production.

The relevance of constructivist aesthetics to the politics of meaning in formulaic art is therefore that significance is not assumed to inhere in any particular element or set of elements; but in the relationships between productive relationships, narrative structure and story told. It is because meaning is continually being accumulated that epic theatre has the funamental attitude of saying 'it can happen this way, but it can also happen quite a different way', there is a distinctive singularity to the performance which should not be overwhelmed by stylistic formulae. This aesthetic is inherently political because it involves asking how communities are accomplished, it starts from the position that the stabilities of folk order cannot be retrieved and therefore meanings are infinitely questionable: 'The idea of man as function of the environment and the environment as a function of man, i.e. the breaking of the environment into relationships between men, corresponding to a new way of thinking, the historical way' (Brecht *op. cit.* p.97). Finally, and to link this discussion back to my opening remarks about the relationship between film and a popular aesthetic, the root metaphor for fictional construction for this aesthetic is the principle of montage: 'i.e. the ability to capture the infinite, sudden or subterranean connections of dissimilars,' (Mitchell's Introduction to Benjamin 1973 p.xiii). In the course of this book I have several times discussed the autonomy of aesthetic experience, meaning the ability of art to exploit its own resources (the knots that hold the edifice together), to identify a perspective that is not specific to an individual. This perspective can masquerade as the viewpoint of 'any reasonable man' and thus reinforce the formula within which it is phrased, or it can invite a comparison between its viewpoint and that of audience members. When the latter process takes place the work that constitutes the art obliterates the distinction between manual and mental labour.

Bibliography

Armes, R. 1974: *Film and Reality.* London: Penguin
Arvon, H. 1973: *Marxist Aesthetics.* Ithaca: Cornell University Press
d'Azevedo, W.L. (ed) 1973: *The Traditional Artist in African Societies.*
    Bloomington: Indiana University Press
Bakhtin, M.M. 1969: *Rabelais and his World.* Cambridge, Mass. MIT Press
Baker, G. 1974: 'Criteria: A New Foundation for Semantics'. *Ratio* 16 (2)
Bann, S. (ed) 1974: *The Tradition of Constructivism.* London: Thames
    and Hudson
Barnouw, E. 1974: *Documentary: A History of the Non-Fiction Film.*
    New York: Oxford University Press
—   1975: *Tube of Plenty.* New York: Oxford University Press
Barr, A.H.Jr, 1975: *Matisse: His Art and his Public.* London: Secker
    and Warburg
Barooshian, V.D. 1975: 'The Aesthetics of the Russian Revolutionary
    Theatre 1917-21'. *British Journal of Aesthetics* 15 (2)
Barthes, R. 1972: *Critical Essays.* Evanston: Northwestern University Press
Battcock, G. (ed) 1975: *Super Realism.* New York: Dutton
Bauman, Z. 1973: *Culture as Praxis.* London: Routledge and Kegan Paul
Becker, E. 1966: *The Birth and Death of Meaning.* New York: Free Press
Becker, H. 1963: *Outsiders.* New York: Free Press of Glencoe
—   1974: 'Art as Collective Action'. *American Sociological Review*
    39 (6)
Benjamin, W. 1970: 'The Work of Art in the Age of Mechanical
    Reproduction'. In *Illuminations,* London: Cape
—   1972: 'A Short History of Photography'. *Screen* 13 (1)
—   1973: *Understanding Brecht.* London: New Left Books
Bensman, J. and Lilienfeld, R. 1971: 'The Journalistic Attitude'. In B.
    Rosenberg and D. White (eds), *Mass Culture Revisited.* New York:
    Van Nostrand
Benthall, J. 1976: *The Body Electric.* London: Thames and Hudson
Berger, J. 1972: *Ways of Seeing.* London: Penguin
Berger, P.L. 1970: 'The Problem of Multiple Realities'. In M. Natanson
    (ed), *Phenomenology and Social Reality.* The Hague: Nijhoff
Berke, J. (ed) 1969: *Counter Culture.* London: Peter Owen Ltd

Betts, R.F. 1971: *The Ideology of Blackness*. Lexington: D.C. Heath

Birnbaum, N. 1969: *The Crisis of Industrial Society*. New York: Oxford University Press

Bloomfield, M.W. (ed) 1970: *The Interpretation of Narration*. Cambridge, Mass.: Harvard University Press

Blum, A. 1974: *Theorizing*. London: Heinemann

Bojko, S. 1972: *New Graphic Design in Revolutionary Russia*. London: Lund Humphries

Boon, J.A. 1973: 'Further Operations of Culture in Anthropology'. In L. Schneider and C. Bonjean (eds), *The Idea of Culture in The Social Sciences*, London: Cambridge University Press

Bourdieu, P. 1973: 'Cultural Reproduction and Social Reproduction'. In R. Brown (ed), *Knowledge, Education and Cultural Change,* London: Associated Publishers

Brecht, B. 1974: 'Against Georg Lukacs'. *New Left Review* 84

Brewster, B. 1974: 'From Shklovsky to Brecht'. *Screen* 15 (2)

Briggs, A. 1960: *Mass Entertainment*. Adelaide: Adelaide University Press

Bruner, J.S., Jolly, A., and Sylva K. (eds) 1976: *Play*. London: Penguin

Bruner, J.S. and Olsen, D. 1973: 'Learning through Experience and Learning through Media'. In G. Gerbner, Gross L., and Melody W. (eds), *Communications, Technology and Social Policy*. New York: Wiley

Burke, K. 1957: *The Philosophy of Literary Form, rev.edn*. New York: Vintage

— 1966: *Language as Symbolic Action*. Berkeley: University of California Press

Burke, P. 1972: *Tradition and Innovation in Renaissance Italy*. London: Batsford

Burns, T. 1973: 'Leisure in Industrial Society'. In M. Smith (ed), *Leisure and Society in Britain*. London: Allen Lane

Cardinal, R. 1972: *Outsider Art*. London: Studio Vista

Carey, J. 1976: 'How Media Shape Campaigns'. *Journal of Communication* 26 (2)

Carter, A. 1967: 'A Theory of Sixties Style'. *New Society* 14 December

Cavendish, P. 1968: 'The Revolution in Culture'. In J. Gray and P. Cavendish (eds), *Chinese Communism in Crisis*. London: Pall Mall

Cawelti, J.G. 1976: *Adventure, Mystery and Romance*. Chicago: Chicago University Press

Chaney, D. 1972: *Processes of Mass Communication*. London: Macmillan

Chatman, S. (ed) 1973: *Approaches to Poetics*. London: Columbia University Press

— 1975: 'Towards a Theory of Narrative'. *New Literary History* vol 6 (2)

Chiang Ching 1968: *On the Revolution in Peking Opera*. Peking: Foreign Languages Press

Christopherson, R. 1974: 'Making Art with Machines'. *Urban Life and Culture* 3 (Apr.)

Clayre, A. 1974: *Work and Play.* London: Weidenfeld and Nicolson

Clark, T.J. 1973: *Image of the People.* London: Thames and Hudson

Cockburn, C. 1972: *Bestseller: The Books that Everyone Read 1900-39.* London: Sidgwick and Jackson

Colby, B.N. and Peacock, J.L. 1973: 'Narrative'. In J.J. Honigmann (ed), *Handbook of Social and Cultural Anthropology,* New York: Rand McNally

Collison, R. 1973: *The Story of Street Literature.* London: Dent

Comfort, A. 1967: *The Anxiety Makers.* London: Nelson

—   1974: 'On Sexuality, Play and Earnest'. *The Human Context* 6

Conrad, P. 1973: *The Victorian Treasure-House.* London: Collins

Colls, R. 1977: *The Collier's Rant.* London: Croom Helm

Crozier, R.C. (ed) 1970: *China's Cultural Legacy and Communism.* London: Pall Mall

Culler, J. 1975: *Structuralist Poetics.* London: Routledge and Kegan Paul

Davidoff, L. 1973: *The Best Circles.* London: Croom Helm

Davis, N.Z. 1975: *Society and Culture in Early Modern France.* Stanford: Stanford University Press

Deak, F. 1975: 'Russian Mass Spectacles'. *Drama Review* 19 (2)

Dondis, D.A. 1973: *A Primer of Visual Literacy.* Cambridge, Mass.: MIT Press

Dorson, R.M. 1971: 'Is there a Folk in the City?'. In A. Paredo and E.J. Stekert (eds), *The Urban Experience and Folk Tradition,* Texas: Texas University Press

Douglas, M. 1975: *Implicit Meanings.* London: Routledge and Kegan Paul

—   1970: *Natural Symbols.* London: Barrie and Jenkins

Duvignaud, J. 1972: *The Sociology of Art.* London: Paladin

Eagleton, T. 1976: 'Criticism and Politics: The Work of Raymond Williams'. *New Left Review* 95

Eisenstein, E.L. 1969: 'The Advent of Printing and the Problem of the Renaissance'. *Past and Present* 45

—   1971: 'Comment and Reply'. *Past and Present* 52

Elias, N. and Dunning, E. 1967: 'The Quest for Excitement in Unexciting Societies'. BSA Conference paper

—   1969: 'The Quest for Excitement in Leisure'. *Society and Leisure* 2

Elliott, P.R.C. 1972: *The Making of a Television Series.* London: Constable

Elliott, P.R.C. and Chaney, D. 1969: 'A sociological framework for the Study of Television Production'. *The Sociological Review* 17 (3)

Ellis, J. 1976: 'Semiology, Art and the Chambers Fallacy'. *Cultural Studies* 9

Fei-Ling (n.d.): *Proletarian Culture in China.* London: Association for Radical East Asian Studies

Fekete, J. 1973: 'McLuhanacy'. *Telos* 15

Fell, J.L. 1974: *Film and the Narrative Tradition*. Oklahoma: Oklahoma University Press

Fernandez, J. 1974: 'The Exposition and Imposition of Order'. In W.L. d'Azevedo (ed), *The Traditional Artist in African Societies*, Bloomington: Indiana University Press

Finnegan, R. 1977: *Oral Poetry*. London: Cambridge University Press

Fisher, P. 1975: 'The Future's Past'. *New Literary History* 6 (3)

Firth, R. 1973: *Symbols: Public and Private*. London: Allen and Unwin

Fitzpatrick, S. 1970: *The Commisariat of Enlightenment 1917-21*. London: Cambridge University Press

Foote, N. 1954: 'Sex as Play'. *Social Problems* 1 (4)

Forge, A. (ed) 1974: *Primitive Art and Society*. London: Oxford University Press

French, P. 1971: *The Movie Moguls*. London: Penguin

Fuglesang, A. 1973: *Applied Communications in Developing Countries* Uppsala: Dag Hammarskjold Foundation

Gans, H.J. 1974: *Popular Culture and High Culture*. New York: Basic Books

Garfinkel, H. and Sacks, H. 1970: 'On Formal Structures of Practical Actions'. In J.C. McKinney and E.A. Tiryakian (eds), *Theoretical Sociology*, New York: Appleton-Century-Crofts

Gay, P. 1976: *Art and Act: On Causes in History*. New York: Harper and Row

Geertz, C. 1972: 'Deep Play: Notes on the Balinese Cockfight' *Daedalus* 101

— 1973: 'Thick Description'. In *The Interpretation of Cultures*. London: Hutchinson

Giddens, A. 1964: 'Notes on the Concepts of Play and Leisure'. *Sociological Review* 12 (1)

Giedion, S. 1960: 'Space Conception in Prehistoric Art'. In E. Carpenter and M. McLuhan (eds), *Explorations in Communication*, Boston: Beacon Press

Goffman, E. 1971: *Relations in Public*. London: Penguin

— 1976a: 'Replies and Responses'. *Language in Society* 5 (2)

— 1976b: 'Gender Advertisements'. *Studies in the Anthropology of Visual Communication* 3 (2)

Golding, J. 1959: *Cubism*. London: Faber and Faber

Gombrich, E. 1974: 'Huizinga and "Homo Ludens" '. *Times Literary Supplement* 4 October, pp.1083-9

— 1975: *Art History and the Social Sciences*. London: Oxford University Press

— 1969: *In Search of Cultural History*. London: Oxford University Press

Goody, J. 1968: *Literacy in Traditional Societies*. London: Cambridge University Press

Goody, J. and Watt, I. 1968: 'The Consequences of Literacy'. In Goody, J. q.v.

Gouldner, A.W. 1976: *The Dialectic of Ideology and Technology.* New York: Seabury Press

Grana, C. 1971: *Fact and Symbol.* New York: Oxford University Press

Grant, D. 1970: *Realism.* London: Methuen

Gray, C. 1970: *The Russian Experiment in Art 1863-1922.* London: Thames and Hudson

Grimes, R.L. 1976: *Symbol and Conquest.* Ithaca: Cornell University Press

Gross, L.P. 1973a: 'Modes of Communication and the Acquisition of Symbolic Competence'. In G. Gerbner *et al.* (eds), *Communications, Technology and Social Policy,* New York: Wiley

—   1973b 'Art as the Communication of Competence'. *Social Science Information* 12 (5)

Hall, S. 1967: 'Leisure, Entertainment and Mass Communication'. BSA Conference Paper

Hall, P.M. and Hewitt, J.P. 1970: 'The Quasi-Theory of Communication and the Management of Dissent'. *Social Problems* 18 (1)

Hanet, K. 1974: 'The Narrative Text of Shock Corridor'. *Screen* 15 (4)

Hao Jan, 1973: 'Why do I write about Workers, Peasants and Soldiers'. *News from Hsinhua* Weekly Issue No. 224

Haralambos, M. 1970 'Soul Music and Blues'. In N.E. Whitten and J.F. Szed (eds) *Afro-American Anthropology* New York: Free Press of Glencoe

Hardy, B. 1975: *Tellers and Listeners.* London: Athlone Press

Harrison, B. 1967: 'Religion and Recreation in Nineteenth Century England'. *Past and Present* 38

Harrison, S. 1974: *Poor Men's Guardians.* London: Lawrence and Wishart

Herrnstein-Smith, B. 1971: 'Poetry as Fiction'. *New Literary History* 2 (2)

—   1976: 'Exchanging Words' unpublished paper

Hess, H. 1975: *Pictures as Arguments.* London: Sussex University Press

Higgins, I. (ed) 1973: *Literature and the Plastic Arts 1880-1930.* Edinburgh: Scottish Academic Press

Hillier, J. 1977: 'Interview with Stanley Donen'. *Movie* 24

Hobsbaum, P. 1970: *A Theory of Communication.* London: Macmillan

Hoggart, R. 1957: *The Uses of Literacy.* London: Chatto and Windus

Hollis, P. 1970: *The Pauper Press.* London: Oxford University Press

Hopcraft, A. 1971: *The Football Man.* London: Penguin

Horkheimer, M. and Adorno, T. 1972: 'The Culture Industry'. In *Dialectic of Enlightenment,* New York: Herder and Herder

Horton, J. 1967: 'Time and Cool People'. *Transaction* 4 (5)

Howard, R. 1971: 'People's Theatre in China since 1907'. *Theatre Quarterly* 1 (4)

Huang, J.C. 1973: *Heroes and Villains in Communist China.* London: Hurst

Huizinga, J. 1971: *Homo Ludens.* London: Paladin

Hyman, L. 1976: ' "The Greek Slave" by Hiram Powers'. *Art Journal* 35 (3)

Hymes, D.H. 1972: 'On Communicative Competence'. In J.B. Pride and J. Holmes (eds), *Sociolinguistics,* London: Penguin

— 1975: 'Breakthrough into Performance'. In D. Ben-Amos and K.S. Goldstein (eds), *Folklore,* The Hague: Mouton

Iser, W. 1975: 'The Reality of Fiction'. *New Literary History* 7 (1)

Ivins, W.M. Jr 1953: *Prints and Visual Communication.* Cambridge, Mass.: Harvard University Press

Jacobs, N. 1961: *Culture for the Millions.* Boston: Beacon Press

Jarvie, I.C. 1970: *Towards a Sociology of the Cinema.* London: Routledge and Kegan Paul

Johnson, R. 1975: 'The Proletarian Novel'. *Literature and History* (2)

Jones, L. 1967: *Black Music.* New York: Morrow

Jussim, E. 1974: *Visual Communication and the Graphic Arts.* New York: R.R. Bowker-Xerox

Kermonde, F. 1972: *Novel and Narrative.* Glasgow: Glasgow University Press

Kinser, B. and Kleinman, N. 1969: *The Dream that was no more a Dream.* New York: Harper and Row

Klingender, F.D. 1972: *Art and the Industrial Revolution.* London: Paladin

— 1975: *Marxism and Modern Art.* London: Lawrence and Wishart

Kristeva, J. 1973: 'The Semiotic Activity'. *Screen* 14 (1/2)

Kunzle, D. 1973: *The Early Comic Strips,* vol. 1. Berkeley: California University Press

Lasch, C. 1976: 'The Narcissist Society'. *New York Review of Books* 23 (15)

Lawson, E.T. 1976: 'Ritual as Language' *Religion* 6 (2)

Laude, J. 1971: *The Arts of Black Africa.* London: California University Press

Leavis, Q.D. 1965: *Fiction and the Reading Public.* London: Chatto and Windus

Lee, D. 1959: *Freedom and Culture.* Englewood Cliffs: Prentice-Hall

Lifschitz, M. 1973: *The Philosophy of Art and Karl Marx.* London: Pluto Press

Lofland, L.H. 1973: *A World of Strangers.* New York: Basic Books

Lomax, A. 1970: 'The Homogeneity of African and Afro-American Musical Style'. In N.E. Whitten and J.F. Szwed (eds), *Afro-American Anthropology.* New York: Free Press and Glencoe

Loos, A. 1974: *Kiss Hollywood Goodbye.* London: W.H. Allen

Lubove, R. 1975: 'Social History and the History of Landscape Architecture'. *Journal of Social History* 9 (2)

Lukacs, G. 1963: *The Meaning of Contemporary Realism.* London: Merlin

MacCabe, C. 1974: 'Realism and the Cinema'. *Screen* 15 (2)

MacCannell, D. 1976: *The Tourist*. London: Macmillan

McCormack, T.M. 1969: 'Folk Culture and the Mass Media'. *European Journal of Sociology* 10 (2)

McKinnon, W.A. 1971: *On the Rise, Progress and Present State of Public Opinion in Great Britain and Other Parts*. Shannon: Irish University Press

McLuhan, M. 1964: *Understanding Media*. London: Routledge and Kegan Paul

—   1967: *Verbi — Voco — Visual Explorations*. New York: Something Else Press

McQuail, D. 1969: *Towards a Sociology of Mass Communications*. London: Collier-Macmillan

Madge, C. and Harrisson, T. 1939: 'A Slight Case of Totemism'. In *Britain by Mass Observation,* London: Penguin.

Malcolmson, R.W. 1973: *Popular Recreations in English Society*. London: Cambridge University Press

Manning, P.K. 1976: 'The Decline of Civility'. *Canadian Review of Sociology* 13 (1)

Mao Tsetung 1967: *On Literature and Art*. Peking: Foreign Language Press

Mayne, J. 1975: 'Eisenstein, Vertov and the Montage Principle'. *The Minnesota Review* (Fall)

Mead, M. 1960: 'Work, Leisure and Creativity. *Daedalus* 89 (1)

Meakin, D. 1976: *Man and Work,* London: Methuen

Mendelsohn, H. 1966: *Mass Entertainment*. New Haven: College and University Press

Merleau-Ponty, M. 1974: *Phenomenology, Language and Sociology*. London: Heinemann

Miller, J. 1971: *McLuhan*. London: Fontana

Mitchell, S. 1974: 'From Schlovsky to Brecht'. *Screen* 15 (2)

Molotch, H. and Lester, M. 1974: 'News as Purposive Behaviour'. *American Sociological Review* 39 (1)

Murdoch, J. 1974: 'English Realism'. *Journal of the Warburg and Courtauld Institute* 37

Murdoch, G. and Golding, P. 1974: 'For a Political Economy of Mass Communications' In *Socialist Register 1973,* London: Merlin

—   1977: 'Capitalism, Communication and Class Relations' in J. Curran (ed), *Mass Communication and Society*. London: Edward Arnold

Musgrove, F. 1974: *Ecstasy and Holiness*. London: Methuen

Mutiso, G.-C. M. 1974: *Socio-Political Thought in African Literature*. London: Macmillan

Nash, J.M. 1974: *Cubism, Futurism and Constructivism*. London: Thames and Hudson

Neuberg, V.E. 1977: *Popular Literature*. London: Penguin

New Literary History 1975: *On Narrative and Narratives*. NLH 6 (2)

Newman, O. 1972: *Defensible Space.* London: Architectural Press

Nochlin, L. 1971: *Realism.* London: Penguin

Obiechina, E. 1975: *Culture, Tradition and Society in the West African Novel.* London: Cambridge University Press

Oliver, P. (ed) 1975: *Shelter, Sign and Symbol.* London: Barrie and Jenkins
— 1976: 'Blue-Eyed Blues'. In C.W.E. Bigsby (ed), *Approaches to Popular Culture,* London: Edward Arnold

Omvedt, G. 1966: 'Play as an Element in Social Life'. *Berkeley Journal of Sociology* 11

O'Neill, J. 1972: 'On Body Politics'. In H.P. Dreitzel (ed), *Recent Sociology* No. 4, New York; Macmillan

Panofsky, E. 1970: *Meaning in the Visual Arts.* London: Penguin

Parker, S. 1975: 'The Sociology of Leisure'. *British Journal of Sociology* 26 (1)

Pateman, T. 1975: *Language, Truth and Politics.* Sidmouth: Stroud and Pateman

Peacock, J.L. 1968: *Rites of Modernization.* Chicago: Chicago University Press

Penn, J.L. 1972: *Linguistic Relativity versus Innate Ideas.* The Hague: Mouton

Petrocci, B. 1976: 'On Urbanity in G. Simmel and R. Musil'. ASA Conference Paper

Poggioli, R. 1968: *The Theory of the Avant-Garde.* Cambridge, Mass.: Harvard University Press

Pollitt, J.J. 1972: *Art and Experience in Classical Greece.* London: Cambridge University Press

Ray, P.C. 1971: *The Surrealist Movement in England.* Ithaca: Cornell University Press

Reilly, M. 1974: *Play as Exploratory Learning.* New York: Sage

Richardson, R. 1969: *Literature and Film.* Bloomington: Indiana University Press

Rosenberg, B. and White, D. 1957: *Mass Culture: the Popular Arts in America.* New York: The Free Press of Glencoe
— 1971: *Mass Culture Revisited.* New York: Van Nostrand

Roskill, M. 1976: *What is Art History?* London: Thames and Hudson

Rossi-Landi, F. 1973: *Ideologies of Linguistic Relativity.* The Hague: Mouton

Rosak, R. 1968: *The Making of a Counter Culture.* New York: Doubleday

Rudé, G. 1971: 'The Pre-industrial Crowd'. In *Paris and London in the Eighteenth-Century.* New York: Viking

Russell, R. 1973: *Bird Lives.* London: Quartet Books.

Sanguineti, E. 1973: 'The Sociology of the Avant-Garde. In E. and T. Burns (eds), *The Sociology of Literature and Drama.* London: Penguin

Sartre, J.P. 1962: *What is Literature?*. New York: Citadel Press

Schapiro, M. 1969: 'On Some Problems in the Semiotics of Visual Art. *Semiotica* 1 (3)

—   1973: *Words and Pictures*. The Hague: Mouton

Schechner, R. 1976: 'Towards a Poetics of Performance'. *Alcheringa* 2 (2)

Scholes, R. 1974: *Structuralism in Literature*. London: Yale University Press

Selden, M. 1971: *The Yenan Way in Revolutionary China*. Cambridge, Mass.: Harvard University Press

Senelick, L. 1975: 'Politics as Entertainment'. *Victorian Studies* 19 (2)

Sennet, R. 1976: *The Fall of Public Man*. New York: Harper and Row

Shepard, L. 1973: *The History of Street Literature*. Newton Abbott: David and Charles

Sheperd, W.C. 1972: 'Religion and the Counter Culture'. *Sociological Inquiry* 42 (1)

Shklovsky, V. 1974: *Mayakovsky and his Circle*. London: Pluto Press

Sigal, L.V. 1973: *Reporters and Officials*. Lexington: R.C. Heath

Silverman, D. 1975: *Reading Castaneda*. London: Routledge and Kegan Paul

Simmel, G. 1971: 'The Metropolis and Mental Life'. In D. Levine (ed), *G. Simmel on Individuality and Social Forms*, London: Chicago University Press

Skorupski, J. 1976: *Symbol and Theory*. London: Cambridge University Press

Smith, A.C.H. Immirzi, E. and Blackwall, T. 1975: *Paper Voices: The Popular Press and Social Change 1935-65*. London: Chatto and Windus

Snow, L.W. 1972: *China on Stage*. New York: Random House

Soyinka, W. 1976: *Myth, Literature and the African World*. Cambridge: Cambridge University Press

Stansill, P. and Mairowitz, D.Z. (eds) 1971: *BAMN*. London: Penguin

Stedman-Jones, G. 1974: 'Working-Class Culture and Working-Class Politics in London 1870-1900'. *Journal of Social History* 7 (4)

Storch, R.D. 1977: 'The Problem of Working Class Leisure'. In A.P. Donajgrodzki (ed), *Social Control in Nineteenth Century Britain*, London: Croom-Helm

—   1976: 'The Policeman as Domestic Missionary'. *Journal of Social History* 9 (4)

Stott, W. 1973: *Real Things Only*. New York: Oxford University Press

Styan, J.L. 1975: *Drama, Stage and Audience*. London: Cambridge University Press

Summary of Forum etc. 1968: *Art and Literature amongst the Armed Forces*. Peking: Foreign Languages Press

Szanto, G.H. 1972: *Narrative Consciousness*. Austin: Texas University Press

Szwed, J.F. 1970: 'Afro-American Musical Adaptation'. Iŋ N.E. Whitten and J.F. Szwed (eds), *Afro-American Anthropology*, New York: Free Press of Glencoe

Tagg, J. 1975: 'The Method of Max Raphael'. *Radical Philosophy* 11

Thomas, K. 1964: 'Work and Leisure in Pre-Industrial Society. *Past and Present* 29

Thompson, E.P. 1971: 'The Moral Economy of the English Crowd in the Eighteenth Century'. *Past and Present* 50

— 1967: 'Time, Work-Discipline and Industrial Capitalism'. *Past and Present* 38

Tudor, A. 1972: 'The Many Mythologies of Realism'. *Screen* 13 (1)

— 1974: *Image and Influence*. London: Allen and Unwin

Tuchman, G. 1973: 'Making News by Doing Work'. *American Journal of Sociology* 79 (1)

Vaughan, D. 1976: *Television Documentary Usage*. BFI Television Monographs No. 6 London

Turner, V. 1973: *Dramas, Fields and Metaphors*. London: Cornell University Press

Vicinus, M. 1974: *The Industrial Muse*. London: Croom-Helm

Vinaver, E. 1971: *The Rise of Romance*. London: Oxford University Press

Vogt, A.M. 1973: *Art of the Nineteenth Century*. London: Weidenfeld and Nicolson

Wallis, R. 1976: 'Moral Indignation and the Media.' *Sociology* 10 (2)

Walton, J.K. 1975: 'Residential Amenity, Respectable Morality and the Rise of the Entertainment Industry'. *Literature and History* 1 (1)

Watson, B.A. 1958: 'Art and Communication'. *Sociology and Social Research* 43 (1)

Watson, W. 1974: *Style in the Arts of China*. London: Penguin

Weider, D.L. and Zimmerman, D.H. 1974: 'Generational Experience and the Rise of Freak Culture.' *Journal of Social Issues* 30 (2)

White, C.L. 1970: *Women's Magazines 1693-1968*. London: Joseph

Willeman, P. 1972: 'On Realisms in the Cinema'. *Screen* 13 (1)

Willett, J. (ed) 1964: *Brecht on Theatre*. London: Eyre Methuen

Williams, R. 1961a: *Culture and Society 1780-1950*. London: Penguin

— 1961b: *The Long Revolution*. London: Chatto and Windus

— 1973: *The Country and the City*. London: Chatto and Windus

— 1974: *Television Technology and Cultural form*. London: Fontana

— 1976: *Keywords*. London: Fontana

— 1977a: *Marxism and Literature*. London: Oxford University Press

— 1977b: 'A Lecture on Realism'. *Screen* 18 (1)

Wilson, H.H. 1961: *Pressure Group*. London: Secker and Warburg

Worth, S. and Gross, L. 1974: 'Symbolic Strategies'. *Journal of Communication* 24 (4)

Wright, L.B. 1935: *Middle-Class Culture in Elizabethan England*. Chapel Hill: University of North Carolina Press

Yale French Studies 1976: *Traditional and Contemporary African Literature*, YFS No. 53

Yao Wenyuan 1968: *Comments on Tao Chu's Two Books*. Peking: Foreign Languages Press

Youngblood, G. 1970: *Expanded Cinema*. New York: Dutton

Zaniello, T.A. 1975: 'Ten Propositions of Contemporary Chinese Aesthetics'. *Minnesota Review* (Fall)

Zurcher, L.A. Jr and Kirkpatrick R.G. 1976: *Citizens for Decency*. Austin: Texas University Press

Index

154 *Index*